COMMENTS ON THE BOOK

BY JOEL C. GREGORY

Preaching is a gift. It cannot be ght.
Preaching has the nature of a sheer ac ners
the gift of preaching and gives those ...urch. Thus,
preaching is a double gift, a gift first to and then a gift of the
preacher to the Church.

In the annals of American preaching, there are examples of that gift given to members of the same family as an act of divine sovereignty. Yet, one family has been given the gift in a conspicuously generous way, the Wade family. It is one thing for several members of a family to mount the pulpit; it is yet another thing for them to do so with abiding excellence, as does the Wade family.

This collection of 15 sermons deserves the oft-overused adjective *unique*. Here, the revered senior nestor of the family of preachers demonstrates the fire that fell in Omaha. Then, his sons in the Spirit and in the flesh show how they picked up the torch lit there and carried it to the next generation.

These are messages of *biblical authority*. Here sounds no uncertain trumpet but the revealed Word of God. These are proclamations of *unusual creativity*. They truly put words of silver into vessels of gold. At the same time, these prophetic pronouncements demonstrate *essential variety*. What a span the preachers cover; from Enoch walking with God to Malcolm X differentiated from Jesus! The sermons are redolent of *actual practicality*. Some preachers soar to the skies above but never land on the earth beneath. These words come from heaven but land on earth. All of these messages demonstrate the mark of proclaimers with *durable maturity*. These are not the sophomoric prattles of untested ministerial novices. These are the substantial works of men whose spiritual experience is self-evident.

Once, the great German preacher Helmut Thielecke said of Spurgeon's sermons, "Sell your shirt if you have to, and get these sermons." Once again, a volume of remarkable homiletic significance has appeared, and I would urge anyone to sell whatever you must or might and have this book. It will inform the layperson, ignite the imagination of the preacher, and convict the cynic. Get it, mark it, use it, and reflect on it. You will be pleased you did.

Joel C. Gregory
Fort Worth, Tex.

Dedication

எலைவை

This book, *These Three, Volume 3,* is dedicated to our father, Dr. J. C. Wade, Sr. and our sister, Doretha Wade-Wilkerson, who are both with our Lord Christ in Heaven.

It was our preaching father who became the preaching paradigm for the Wade family. What was so interesting about our father was the fact that he grew up an orphan and because of poverty, he graduated from the eighth grade at the age of seventeen. Though he was an orphan and finished the eighth grade at the age of seventeen, he did not allow these disadvantages to deter him, but he used them as fulcrums to propel him to a level of preaching excellence. In spite of his disadvantages, he is now known for being a classic evangelical doctrinal Jesus preacher and for his classic "runs".

We, also, include on this dedication page our sister Doretha, who was the musical genius of the family. From the time that she was sixteen, she gave dynamic music leadership until God took her home to be with Him. She will always be remembered for the all time classic gospel song, "I Don't Feel Noways Tired" as she directed the Salem Choir teaming with the late Rev. James Cleveland.

So we dedicate this third volume to these two giants.

Thank You

We would like to say on this Thank You page that we say thank you to Dr. Richard (Dean) Rollins for once again doing his unusual and exceptional best in editing our manuscripts. Dean, it is evident that you are the best; we owe you so much, and we say thank you.

We would, also, like to say thank you to Tina Carter of the Mt. Moriah Baptist Church for working with Dr. Rollins so tirelessly in order to do the final renderings of our manuscripts.

Furthermore, we would like to thank Pamela Johnson and Essie Jenkins of Mt. Moriah Baptist Church and Deana Johnson of the Zion Missionary Baptist Church for their contributions as they did the original transcribing of our works. Ladies, all four of you, we cannot say thank you enough as you do such a monumental job in deciphering our hieroglyphics.

THESE THREE
VOL. 3

By
Dr. J. C. Wade, Sr.
Dr. M. V. Wade, Sr.
Dr. J. C. Wade, Jr.

These Three, Volume 3

Copyright © 2005 by The R.H. Boyd Publishing Corporation

6717 Centennial Blvd.

Nashville, TN 37209-1049

ISBN 1-58942-311-9

Printed in the United States of America

TABLE OF CONTENTS

ENOCH WALKED WITH GOD

Genesis 5:24; Hebrews 11:5

The Bible does not present a more saintly character than Enoch. Both Genesis and Hebrews testify to the fact that his distinguishing mark was that he walked with God. No greater compliment can be paid to any man, neither can a more beautiful epitaph be engraved upon a stone of marble to mark one's final resting place than that he walked humbly with God.

Here was a man in the early childhood of the world, who distinguished himself by the simple, noticeable, and commendable act of daily walking with God. He did not put on any hypocritical airs, nor did he shout his righteousness from high hills or from house to house. He did not carry a sign on his back to publicize to the community his intimate relationship with God.

He made no public display to receive the applause of his countrymen and friends. He did not ask about the public's opinion concerning his devotion to God. He sought no honors and he garnered no laurels for himself. He coveted no lofty station; he sought no praises from his contemporaries; he laid no claim to fame; and he sought no spotlight. His name never appeared in lights, and he never mentioned his holiness. He held no office among the city fathers, nor had any pull with the affluent.

Nothing is said about his social standing. Nothing is said about his riches, nor did he ride in pomp and splendor. He was not a show-off, and there was no king's crown which adorned his brow. He did not sway a king's scepter over a province, and no subjects bowed at his feet in reverence to him.

No jumping chariot drawn by prancing horses carried him wherever he desired to go. He did not live in a palatial mansion, and he was not a people-pleaser. He was not swayed by the crowd, nor was he influenced by his ungodly peers. Enoch just walked with God. He walked with God for the joy of walking with Him. He walked with God, for it was a privilege to walk. He walked with God for the pleasure of walking with Him. He walked with God because of the glorious fellowship.

Enoch did not know that, in the centuries to come, his name would be inscribed upon the sacred pages of the Holy Bible. He did not know that twentieth century preachers and teachers would be preaching and teaching about his godly life. He just walked with God. He walked with God because he loved God. He walked with God because he found joy in God.

This primitive man had something deep down on the inside of him that this modern-day crowd needs, needs worse than anything else; and that is a soul consciousness of God and a new birth which will give them an experimental knowledge of God. This present-day crowd needs to know God intimately. This is what our world needs, not in mass but individually.

There is no such thing as walking with God if one does not know God. There is no such thing as walking with God if one does not love God. There are some who do not believe in God; however, this does not affect God in the least. God will still be God if never another sinner bows at His feet. There are those who say that, if there be a God, He has surely secluded Himself and is only concerned with the natural world and order of things. This is not so. God is still in control of His world and everything in it.

The story is told of an atheist who said to the minister, "Sir! If there is a God, let Him strike me dead in twenty minutes." The minister, knowing God as he did, said, "Sir! You cannot exhaust God's patience in twenty minutes. You see, God is real. He is no phantom. He is not a figment of the human imagination. What we know and what is said about Him by those of us who know him is no ghost story. God is real."

This is what Enoch knew. Enoch knew God personally, and God knew Enoch intimately. He knew God as the eternal, self-existent God, who is God all by Himself. God was Enoch's constant companion. God and Enoch were close friends. They walked and talked with each other as friends. Enoch could depend on God, and God could depend on Enoch. Enoch trusted God, and God trusted Enoch. He knew that God was concerned with nature, but it was not enough to satisfy Enoch. Nothing satisfied him but a day-to-day fellowship, and daily communion with God. Enoch was not a put-on nor a show-off. Enoch was real in his religion. He was happy with God, and God was pleased with him. He was happy walking with God, and God enjoyed having Enoch's company and conversations.

For three hundred years, Enoch walked with God. Every step drew him closer to God. Their every conversation grew sweeter and sweeter as the days, weeks, months, and years rolled by. As Enoch went about from day to day, tending sheep, plowing his field, planting his crops, gathering his harvest, herding his cattle, and directing and guiding his family in the way of right, God was uppermost in his mind. His occupation of the day did not disturb Enoch in the least as it related to his walk with God.

He knew that God was the only source of life. He knew that God was the only joy in life. He was not on and off with God. Every day with Enoch was God's day. Every hour of the day with Enoch was God's hour. Every minute was God's minute with Enoch. His every move was God-ward, and his every desire was to please God. His every waking moment was spent with God, and his whole life was wrapped up and tied up in God.

His every endeavor was directed by God, and he dedicated his all to God. Nothing was as important to him as God. His delight was to commune with God. He knew that, in God, he lived and moved and had his being. He knew that all that was worth having came to him from God. Unkind words were said to him. Ugly things were said about him. His familiar friends deserted him. Enoch had his high hills and mountains to climb. He had his rough roads to travel, and he had his crosses to bear. He had his heavy loads to carry, and, at times, his days were dark. At times, his nights were long and dreary. At times, he had no song to sing, day nor night. Sometimes, his sleep broke from him. Sometimes, he went with a broken heart. His path of life was not strewn with flowers all the way.

Not everyone who patted him on the back was his friend. Not everyone who congratulated him was sincere. But through it all, Enoch was determined deep in his heart to make it. He walked humbly with God, and no man could make him break his stride.

Enoch is a perfect example for Christians today. We must determine in our hearts to make it. There is nothing worthwhile to turn back about. But what does it mean to walk with God? It means, first of all, an experiential knowledge of God or being born again. It means repentance toward God and the exercise of simple faith in the death, burial, resurrection, and ascension of Jesus. It means exercising simple faith in the cleansing, saving, justifying, sanctifying power of His own precious blood which was shed on Calvary. This does not mean that we are immune to temptations.

No man ever escapes temptations. No man is strong enough in himself to resist temptations. No man is too holy for Satan to attack, and no man is so pure that Satan will refuse to try to defile him. No man can have so much religion that Satan refuses to try to disgrace him. No man is so good that Satan will refuse to try to seduce him. No man has so much religion that Satan will refuse to try to entice him.

You see, we are never so strong as Christians that we can make it on our own. The human will is so weak, and the human passion is so easily ignited that, in hours of temptation, the strongest Christian weakens without the strengthening power and guidance of the Holy Spirit. Paul writes, "Let him that thinks he stands, beware, lest he falls."

In this life, we who are Christians must walk in the fear of God with trembling steps. Walking with God involves so much. It involves love, kindness, gentleness, meekness, Christian sympathy, goodness, brotherly concern, a bridled tongue, a pure heart, a humble spirit, a clear conscience, a clean mind, an outstretched arm to help, a forgiving spirit, mercifulness, patience, faith, cross bearing, thankfulness, honorableness, being knowledgeable, honest, truthful, obedient, dependable, watchful, law-abiding, peacemaking, doing good works, exemplary in deportment, no ears to listen to idle gossip, and no tongue for slandering another.

Walking with God includes being spirit filled, worshiping God in the Lord's house, exemplifying zeal for the Lord's work, a yearning for the Lord's house, a will to do the Lord's bidding, demonstrating pleasure in obeying the Lord's commands, complete trust in the Lord's Word, sincerity in doing the Lord's business, faithfulness to the Lord's cause, responsible as the Lord's steward, unselfishness, courteous in speech, a friendly smile, a hearty handshake, not being deceitful, sharing with others, being gentle and temperate, long-suffering, vigilant, thoughtful, diligent in all things, compassionate, keeping the peace, not double-tongued, not being a striker, not easily provoked, not being a brawler, a lover of the good, prayerful at all times, studious in the Word, constant in worship, grateful, watchful, reasonable, devout, graceful, serviceable, trustworthy, and forbearing.

It involves being as wise as a serpent and harmless as a dove. It involves thinking wholesome thoughts, doing good deeds, loving and feeding the enemy, going the second mile, having a sweet disposition, having the right attitude, harboring no hate, carrying no grudges, reliable, witty, ingenious, industrious, likable, lovable, competent, prudent, gracious, serious, cordial, brave, and bold.

It involves being on fire for God, being appreciative, endurance, inner strength, sobriety, foresightedness, discretion, agreeable, dedication, consecration, determination, being constructive.

It involves communication, a cheerful attitude, charitableness, being alert, admirable, accountable, self-denying, accommodating, considerate of others, and always abounding in the work of the Lord. These and more were the characteristics of the man Enoch.

The Bible has much to say to us who are determined to walk with God. The Bible says to walk in the light. Walk while you have light. Walk while you have the light of life. Walk while you have the light of lights. Walk in the old path. Walk in the good way. Walk in the Lord's statutes. Walk in the Lord's commandments. Walk in the Lord's testimonies. Walk in the Lord's favor. Walk before the Lord with a perfect heart. Walk before the Lord in peace with all men. Walk before the Lord in the beauty of holiness. Walk before the Lord in truth. Walk before the Lord in righteousness. Walk with the Lord with a melody in your heart. Walk in the law of the Lord. Walk in the way that is well-pleasing to God, and walk with your mind stayed on God. Walk in the way which the Lord has chosen. Walk after the Lord. Walk in the path of the just. Walk in the name of the Lord. Walk in the company of the upright. Walk in the newness of life. Walk according to God's rule. Walk in the way of Jesus Christ. Walk after the Spirit. Walk in the Spirit.

Walk in the way of the Spirit's leading. Walk by the Word of the Lord. Walk with spiritual integrity. Walk with the lowly Nazarene. Walk and not faint. Walk not in the counsel of the ungodly. Walk not in the way of the unclean. Walk before the Lord with a pure heart. Walk in the path of the just. Walk as it becometh godliness. Walk not in the way of Jeroboam. Walk with hope, in trust, and in peace. Walk with reverence, and walk in sincerity. Walk with trembling and fear and not with faltering steps. Walk humbly with thy God. Walk circumspectly in the world. Walk tall in Gospel shoes. Walk erect, having your loins girded with the truth. Walk unafraid, hanging onto the breastplate of eternal salvation. Walk not disorderly. Let your words be seasoned with salt. Always speak highly of others. Owe no man anything but love. Never be a talebearer. Be as kind as you can to everyone. Be mindful of the poor. Help those in need.

Let a brother's load be your load. Possess a quiet spirit. Do all you can do for others, and don't brag about it. This was Enoch's life. This was his badge of distinction. He walked with God three hundred years. You do not have to write a book to tell whether a man has lived a noble life or wasted it. The words of the text tell of the life of Enoch. He walked with God.

These four words are a great testimony for Enoch. In spite of his foes, he walked with God. In spite of harsh criticism, he walked with God. In spite of unbelievers, he walked with God. In the face of stiff opposition, he walked humbly with God. When friends turned away from him, he walked humbly with God. Day by day, week by week, month by month, and year by year, Enoch kept step with God. He taught the world not by words but by his daily life.

One year passed; two years passed; ten years went by; fifty years went by; one hundred years passed by; two hundred years sped by; three hundred and then he was not, for God took him. In the prime of life, he kept step with God and afterwards walked so close to God that death did not even come close to him. You see, heaven is but the continuation of a holy walk with God on earth. Enoch's departure proves that there is a heaven, a land of pure delight, a land of eternal bliss, a land where saints immortal reign, a land of joy and peace.

FREE, BUT NOT CHEAP

John 10:28

I have often said that, if eternal life could be bought with money, all men would try to buy it. Money or no money, regardless of the cost, even on credit with an agreement to pay the debt week by week or in monthly installments, we can't buy it because it is free.

Many men would even mortgage their choice possessions to borrow enough money and pay it back with interest, even compound interest, if eternal life could be bought with money. You can't buy it; it is free.

If we work hard for it, we would spend each waking hour on the job trying to earn it, but it is free. If we had to work for eternal life a lifetime, that would not be long enough to earn enough money to make the first down-payment. It is free. If we had to buy it, how could we estimate its eternal value in terms of dollars and cents, even if we had a computer at our finger-tips? If we had to earn it, what job would we have to work on day and night to make the first installment? If we had to study for it, what university would we attend? What textbooks would we use? Who would be our instructors? How many credit hours would we have to take? How many years of study would we have to put in? When could we hope to graduate?

If we had to study for eternal salvation, our bookshelves would be over-crowded with books, and we would burn the midnight oil preparing for the test, but it is free. If we had to search for life, we would search in every crack, crevice, and cranny to find it, but it is free.

From the lips of Jesus come these words, "I give unto them eternal life, and they shall never perish." He gave it freely, with no strings attached. Jesus said that it is a free gift. It is free to all men of every language, kindred, and tongue, just for the act of simple faith. I hold that this is the reason so many people miss it. Because it is free, people can't see it and never lay hold on it. It is hard for people to see how the eternal God can freely give eternal life to unworthy, undeserving sinners without a price tag being hung on it, but I tell you again that it is free.

Men are so mercenary that they feel anything that is worth anything ought to cost something. Earthly men think earthly thoughts. All they see is that which is earthly. They measure a man by the cost of his clothes, his house, his car, and his bank account. They value everything in terms of money. They are moved by the dollar sign. They feel that, if it doesn't cost anything, it isn't worth anything. But years ago, I heard this true statement,

"The best things in life are free." The best things in life are free, and I know it is true, for the best thing in life to have is eternal life and it is free.

It is not to be gained by works, bought with money, attained by constant study, nor found by diligent search. It is the free gift from God by Jesus Christ. Jesus said that it is free for all who exercise a saving faith in Him. From the prophecy of Isaiah, chapter 55, comes the great invitation: "Ho, everyone that thirsteth, come ye to the waters, and he that hath no money; come ye, buy, and eat; yea, come, buy wine and milk without money and without price. Wherefore do ye spend money for that which is not bread? and your labor for that which satisfieth not? hearken diligently unto me, and eat ye that which is good, and let your soul delight itself in fatness. Incline your ear, and come unto me. ... and I will make an everlasting covenant with you, even the sure mercies of David ... Seek ye the Lord while he may be found, call ye upon him while he is near: Let the wicked forsake his way, and the unrighteous man his thoughts: and let him return unto the Lord, and he will have mercy upon him; and to our God, for he will abundantly pardon."

No amount of gold, silver, currency, or sparkling jewels can be used to estimate the value nor pay the price for eternal life. If we wanted to buy it, how would we go about estimating its earthly and its eternal worth? What figure would we use? What would be our highest bid? If we tried to estimate the value of eternal life in round figures of dollars, our arms would drop to our sides, and our bodies would become completely exhausted as we add zeros to zeros futilely to determine its worth.

If we stacked currency mountain high for a price of eternal life, it would not be high enough for the down payment. If we weighed all of the gold and silver and costly jewels in the world together, they would not come up to the worth of eternal life here and hereafter. It is free.

The human eyes would go blind from reading books if one tried to study the height, depth, length, breadth, and duration of eternal life. This leads me to say again that it is free. And again, the best thing in life is free—eternal life!

If the best things in life are not free, tell me, how do we estimate the value of a mother's love? What price tag do we hang on her devotion? What about a father's toiling day and night for his family? What cost price do we have on that? How much in cold cash is one minute of time worth? How do we estimate the value of life itself? How much is one day worth? How many millions of dollars do we pay for just being alive?

Can we put a dollar sign on health and strength? How much do we pay for the blood that is pumped through our veins and arteries? What is the price of one heartbeat? What price tag hangs on our eyesight and hearing? What about the movement of our muscles and activity of our limbs? What is the price of our gift of speech? Can we figure out the worth of a night's sleep? Do we get a bill for sunshine? How much do we pay for the cool breeze that blows on our mortal frame? What about our brilliant mind? Does a collector come by to collect for the power of thought?

All of these things and many more are free. No man can estimate their value. As no man can estimate the value of these things, so it is when it comes to estimating the value of eternal life. Trying to put a price tag on these things is like trying to hang one on the solar system. As no man can measure the depth of man's fall, no man can measure the depth of God's love for man and man's immortal soul, nor can man hang a price tag on his redemption through and by Jesus Christ, who shed His blood on Calvary, nor on eternal life by our exercise of simple faith in Him.

You see, eternal life for man is God's work from beginning to end. I often say that God thought it in eternity, eons before the world was framed by His eternal Word, and Christ perfected it on Calvary. He offers it to all men— free. This giving of eternal life was preconceived in the Divine Mind, in the Determinate Council of the Godhead, long before Adam's fall in Eden. Therefore, since man's fall was foreknown by God, it is unthinkable that world redemption and eternal life for man was an afterthought of God. Had man's fall been unknown to God, it would have shocked Him and taken Him by surprise. But since all is foreknown to God, nothing is a surprise to God. From all eternity, He knows all things to eternity which is to come. God knew in eternity, according to His omniscience, that weak and sinning men would need a merciful and loving Savior. God knew that the more man tried to make himself right after his fall, the more ridiculous, shameful, and unworthy he would become. Thus, He took the initiative to provide a way that would save man and restore him back to that relationship with Himself when He created him.

As we scan the pages of the Old Testament, we soon discover that God's voice was heard through sages and prophets across the centuries concerning man's fall and world redemption by and through the precious blood of Christ. The following descriptions attest to God's voice in the Old Testament.

Job, the man of patience.

Abraham, the father of many nations and a man of undaunted faith.

Isaac, the beloved husband of Rebekah.

Jacob, the father of Israel.

Moses, the leader of Israel.

Joseph, the prisoner of Egypt.
Joshua, the successor to Moses.
Caleb, the faithful follower of Moses.
Elijah, the prophet of fire.
Elisha, the spiritual son of Elijah.
Samuel, the saintly judge of Israel.
Jehu, who wiped out Ahab, Jezebel, and their posterity.
Josiah, the youngest king of Israel.
Ezra, the ready scribe in Israel.
David, the shepherd king of Israel.
Solomon, the sage of the ages.
Nehemiah, who rebuilt the walls of Jerusalem.
Amos, the prophet of social justice.

All of these, with the rest of the major and minor prophets, looked forward to the day when the Christ would come and redeem the world with His own precious blood and would triumph over death, hell, and the grave, and arise King of kings and Lord of lords. Malachi, standing amid the dust of a night which was to be four hundred years long, saw Christ coming as the sun of righteousness, with healing in His wings. David, having served his generation well, fell asleep while looking for the coming of his Good Shepherd.

Zechariah wrote saying, "Rejoice greatly, O daughter of Zion; shout, O daughter of Jerusalem: behold, thy King cometh unto thee: he is just, and having salvation." This is the truth upon which the prophets staked their hopes. This is the truth that bolstered their courage. With such a predetermined plan for world redemption and the giving of life eternal to all who believe, it is no wonder that John the Baptist, the wilderness preacher who came too late to call himself a prophet and too soon to be numbered with the apostles, deduced his entire being in words and labeled himself just as the voice of one crying in the wilderness.

John had no message of his own to give, for he had no eternal life to offer. He had no undying love to demonstrate. He had no mercy to show. He had no heart big enough to pity all mankind. He had no saving grace to bestow, and he had no life of his own to give to another. In fact, John was not present when the scheme of redemption was worked out by the Divine Mind. Had he been there, the plan of redemption and how it would work would have been too deep for John to comprehend. John knew the sin problem, but, being human, John knew not how to solve it. He knew that man needed saving but knew not how to save him. He knew that man was lost but knew now how man could be found. He knew that man was wrecked but knew now how to repair the damage.

John knew that man was vile, wretched, dirty, filthy, and unclean but knew not how to cleanse him. He knew that man was a wanderer but knew not how to bring him back into fellowship with God. He knew that man was sin-sick, from head to foot, but had no remedy for his sickness. He knew that man was out of harmony with God but knew not how to bring about harmony between them. But God knew how to fix it all.

The psalmist was right when he said, "The Lord is my light and my salvation." Jonah reminds us that that there is nothing in us that merits salvation, but rather salvation is of the Lord. You see, the price for eternal life was too much for mortal man to pay. It had to be paid by One who had life in Himself. It had to be paid by One who is the giver of life. Jesus said Himself, "I came that they might have life." I came that they might have the light of life. I came that they might have the full life. I came that they might have abundant life. I came that they might have everlasting life, and I came to give them eternal life.

We cannot estimate the value of mortal life; therefore, we are incompetent to estimate the value of eternal life. Our lives here are transitory. Our days are fleeting, and our days are numbered. Just one quick swing of the pendulum of the clock of time, and we are no more. Just a few rising and setting suns, and our sojourn here on earth is over. Just a few days of happiness with our families, and our chairs are left vacant.

But here in the text, Jesus offers eternal life. He offers life without an end. He offers life here and in the hereafter. He offers life that will never know sickness. He offers life that will never know pain. He offers life that will never know sorrow. He offers life that will never know death. The life He gives does not end at the deathbed. The life He gives does not end in the grave. This life is free, but let us not suppose that it is cheap. It is free but not cheap. Heaven went to too much expense to call it cheap. It cost God more to redeem the world and save us than it did when He created the world.

The making of the world only cost God His breath, but the perfecting of the plan of salvation and giving to us eternal life cost Him His Son, Jesus Christ. "God gave us the very best He had. The Father gave His Son; the Father gave His son for me. One day when I was lost, He died upon the cross. The father gave His Son for me.

The Son gave His life; the Son gave His life; the Son gave His life for me. One day when I was lost, He died upon the cross, the Son gave His life for me." Through His shed blood on Calvary, Jesus gives us life, and the life He gives is eternal.

Note the invitation. Come while the table is spread. Come while the light of hope still shines. Come to the feast. Come now. Now is the accepted time. Come while you have time. Come while mercy's doors are open. Come before it is too late. Come while the Spirit pleads. Come to the Master's call. Come at the Gospel invitation. Behold, now is the day of salvation. Come to the wedding feast. Come while you have your right mind. Seek ye the Lord while He may be found. Call ye upon Him while He is near.

If we confess our sins, He is faithful and just to forgive us and cleanse us from all our sins. If thou shall confess with thy mouth the Lord Jesus, and shall believe in thine heart that God has raised Him from the dead, thou shall be saved. He that believeth on the Son hath everlasting life. I give unto them eternal life, and they shall never perish.

"'Tis a sweet and glorious thought that comes to me.
I'll live on, yes, I'll live on.
Jesus saved my soul from death, and now I'm free.
I'll live on, yes, I'll live on.

When my body's sleeping in the cold, cold clay,
I'll live on, yes, I'll live on.
There to sleep in Jesus 'til the judgment day.
I'll live on, yes, I'll live on.

In the glory land, with Jesus on the throne,
I'll live on, yes, I'll live on.
Through eternal ages, singing home sweet home,
I'll live on, yes, I'll live on.

I'll live on, yes, I'll live on.
Through eternity, I'll live on.
I'll live on, yes, I'll live on.
Through eternity, I'll live on."

GRUMBLING ABOUT GRACE

Matthew 20:1-16

Our text grows out of a reply that Jesus made to Simon Peter, and Simon Peter's statement was an aftermath of Jesus' parable about "the rich young ruler." After Jesus gives the parable about "the rich young ruler," Peter said, in essence, "you told the rich young man to sell all he had and follow you. And, that's exactly what we have done. We have left everything and followed you; what shall we have therefore?" Simon was saying, "Lord, unlike the young man who did not leave his possessions, we did not trust in our possessions; we left them and we have trusted you and staked our existence upon you; we have given up our diverse vocations; we have sacrificed our families and homes, we have abandoned all for your sake. Now what we need to know is, for all of this trusting, abandoning, and renouncing, what is to be our gain?" Peter was dealing in the area of remuneration. In response to Peter's inquiry, Jesus tells a picturesque parable. The main subject matter of this parable is that Kingdom remuneration is given but not earned, which makes it grace. Whatever things they had forsaken for the Kingdom were not really sacrifices, but they were investments with guaranteed dividends for this life and the life to come.

Jesus begins the parable by saying, "early in the morning," probably about 6:00 a.m., which was the beginning of the Jewish day, a landowner went to the marketplace or labor exchange to hire laborers.

In the ancient east, hired laborers were considered to be near the bottom of the socio-economic scale; they were not far above beggars.

The Bible says something interesting, and that is that not his steward but the landowner himself went and found the lowest class of workers in the marketplace. He began the search at 6:00 a.m. Upon finding these hired laborers at 6:00 a.m., the landowner strikes a bargain with these hired laborers. Now, the Bible does not say that the hired laborers insisted on making a verbal contract, but it does imply it. For, in verse 13, the landowner asked, "Didn't you agree to work for a denarius?" And then, in verse 2, it states, "He agreed to pay them a denarius for the day," which was the wage of a Roman soldier and about 15 to 20 cents in our modern currency for a day's work. The Bible says that later on, at 9:00 a.m., 12 noon, and 3:00 p.m., not the steward but the landowner returns to the marketplace to hire more laborers. Once again, he strikes a bargain with these hired laborers. But notice, this time, he does not bargain with these laborers concerning any set wages, he only agrees to pay them "whatsoever is right."

Then finally, at the eleventh hour, or about 5:00 p.m., just an hour before sunset, the landowner returns to the marketplace to find other laborers. When the landowner arrives back at the marketplace, he finds workers with forlorn or desperate hopes. Upon seeing these hopeless men, the landowner asked them why they were not working. They responded by saying, "Because no man hath hired us."

At the eleventh hour, the landowner gave those eleventh-hour men some work to do. Once again, the landowner strikes a bargain and agrees to pay them "whatsoever is right."

At this point, all of the workers in the marketplace are now in the vineyard frantically racing against time. Keep in mind now that all of the workers have gone into the vineyard at varied intervals. Remember too, that there are two groups. One group is the group on a fixed contract; the other group are the laborers who are just glad to have work, and they have the promise of the landowner to do "whatsoever is right." To be more specific, the first group is the hired, and the second group is the called.

At the evening, the owner of the vineyard instructs his steward to pay off the workers. To pay off the workers at evening time was in keeping with the Mosaic law. Because of God's great compassion for the poor and downtrodden, the Mosaic law stated that hired laborers should not have their wages deferred until tomorrow, but they should receive them with the going down of the sun.

It is now that we encounter further radical action on the part of the landowner. For some unmentioned reason, the steward is instructed by the landowner to begin the payoff by starting with the last laborers first. Again, for some unmentioned reason, each one of the last laborers received a penny, or a denarius, which was the same amount of money that he had promised to give to those who went to work at 6:00 a.m. Upon seeing the generosity of the owner, those who had gone to work earlier started calculating and anticipated 12 days pay for one day of work. However, to their dismay, they too received a denarius. Upon receiving what they agreed to, their hopes were dashed. They became exceedingly disgruntled at perceived injustice. As a result, after they had taken the money, they did something that church people do now which the Bible never commends or condones, but condemns, and that is, they murmured. In their murmuring, they registered the complaint that the other men had worked a shorter time span. They complained that some of the other workers entered the tasks when it was the cool of the evening. They complained that it was them who had born the burden of the work and scorching heat of the mid-day sun. The Bible says that "they murmured against the goodman of the house."

Let's look closer at this story. The first thing that we want to look at is:

I. The Generous Master

When you look at verses 1, 3, 5, and 6 and then put this story in its proper context, you come to see that the master of the house was compelled by grace to go to the marketplace. When you understand the fact that the owner of the vineyard symbolizes God the Father, then you come to understand that, even though we are talking about a frantic race against time because it is autumn, which makes it the rainy season and grape harvest time, the fact of the matter is, the context is not really about a frantic race against time for the ingathering of grapes, but it is about meeting the frantic and desperate needs of men.

When you look at the fact that the owner went to the marketplace five different times, you come to see that he hired them not because of his need, but he hires them because of their frantic need.

The Bible depicts man as a creature in desperate need and Jehovah Jireh as a need-meeting God. Matthew 6:8 says, "Your Father knoweth what things ye have need of, before ye ask Him." Philippians 4:19 says, "But my God shall supply all your need according to His riches in glory by Christ Jesus."

To show you that, first of all, Jehovah Jireh is a God who is graciously aware of our needs, look at the fact that, in the Book of Isaiah, chapter 6, we find God seated on a throne of infinite majesty and holiness. That makes the throne a throne of awe. Then, in Revelation, chapter 6, we find God sitting on His throne as the God of wrath and judgment. That makes the throne a throne of terror. But God, knowing that man in his sinful condition could not handle either coming to the throne of awe or the throne of terror, but desperately and frantically needed to approach the throne, at an infinite cost to Himself, has transformed that throne of awe and terror, and now that throne is a throne of grace. That's why Hebrews 4:16 says, "Let us therefore come boldly unto the throne of grace, that we may obtain mercy, and find grace to help in time of need." God is a God who is graciously aware of our needs, but when you look contextually, you will see secondly that God is not just graciously aware of our needs, but He is a God who meets our needs. And, God would rather meet our needs on one basis, and that basis is the basis of grace.

Let me just say parenthetically that, when we compare this text with Hebrews 4:16, we come to see at least two phases of grace. In the text, we see grace being an unmerited favor, but when we look at Hebrews 4:16, we see grace as God's enabling power. When we sing, "Grace woke me up this morning," that's grace as an unmerited favor, but then we sing, "Grace started me on my way," that's grace as enabling power. Together they represent grace for our unworthiness and our inadequacies.

The fact then is, since grace deals with our unworthiness and our inadequacies, like these last workers, we have only one thing to do, and that is trust in God's grace alone. But, I'm coming to find out that the most difficult task for us is to rely on God's grace alone. It appears that our pride won't let us rest on grace alone. Somehow, we believe that, if we live on grace alone, we would have to live on a kind of celestial welfare system. So, because of our pride, we want to do like these first workers; we want 50 percent performance and 50 percent grace. That means that we dichotomize the Christian life into grace and works. But, I'm here to tell us that grace is not a works plus grace relationship. When we talk grace, we are not talking about grace supplementing our good works. Grace is not about making up for what we lack. If we think grace is about supplement, then we don't understand grace because grace has nothing to do with us. Grace is about God's infinite, generous goodness; God's sovereign purpose; and the eternal, justice-satisfying merits of Christ. There is an acronym for grace which is, "God's Riches at Christ's Expense." If grace took us into account, we would never have grace because all grace would see is fallen, ruined, depraved, unworthy, sinful, guilty, ill-deserving, and bankrupt sinners, deserving retributive justice. So, what grace does is look away from us and see the eternal merits of Jesus Christ, and based upon the eternal merits of Christ, God bestows grace upon us for our unworthiness and our inadequacies. But then, we sing "His grace is sufficient." So, to say that "His grace is sufficient" is an open admission that what we inherently possess is insufficient.

Then, when we look at the master paying off at the end of the day, and especially the eleventh hour workers, we see that God's rewards are always out of proportion to our finite efforts. God is an exceedingly and infinitely generous God. The story is told about a Sunday School teacher who asked her Sunday School students if they knew the difference between kindness and loving-kindness. One little girl said that she knew the difference. She told the teacher that kindness is like when you ask your mother for some toast and she gives it to you, but loving-kindness is when you ask your mother for some toast and she gives you toast with some jelly on it. And, that's the way God is. God, in His loving-kindness, is an exceedingly generous giver. He doesn't just give you some blessings, but He gives you some blessings with some jelly on it.

That's why the Bible says that "He daily loadeth us with benefits." He is exceedingly generous. David says, "He anointeth my head with oil, my cup runneth over." He is exceedingly generous. God says, "Bring the whole tithe into the storehouse, and I will open the windows of heaven and pour you out blessings that you won't have room to receive." God is exceedingly generous. Jesus said, "Give and it shall be given to you good measure, pressed down, shaken together and running over." The Bible says that Jesus fed a multitude of 5,000 besides women and children with two fishes and five loaves of bread, and there were 12 baskets left. God is an exceedingly generous God.

In Matthew 19:29, Jesus said, "Every one that hath forsaken houses, or brethren, or sisters, or father, or mother, or wife, or children, or lands, for my name's sake, shall receive an hundredfold, and shall inherit everlasting life." Now, a hundredfold is 10,000 percent. God is exceedingly generous. And, because God is exceedingly generous, His rewards are always out of proportion to our finite efforts.

This ought to challenge us to live by grace alone.

Secondly, let's look at:

II. The Jealous Murmurers

Understand that the murmurers represent believing disciples who suffered from spiritual jaundice and parochialism, and that is jealous prejudice and spiritual narrowness.

In keeping this story in its proper perspective, this parable was directed to Simon Peter and the rest of the disciple band. The disciples, undoubtedly, had gotten the impression that, since they had come into the Kingdom right at its very inception at the ground floor, they should have greater Kingdom remuneration. This says that they had a self-serving merit mentality. They were in danger of doing the Lord's work and yet not doing His will from the heart. They were in danger of serving the Lord for temporal benefits and missing the best blessings.

Now, these first workers were descriptive of some believing disciples then, but they are also descriptive of some believing disciples now.

There is a word that pervades our society that is so detrimental to us. The word is *entitlement*. Now, the word *entitlement* might be alright for secularism or in the workforce, but spiritually, it is presumptuous. It carries the presumptuous idea of working your way to where you deserve, or merit something better. From the Kingdom side, nobody works their way to the level of deserving something better because, at best, all of our good works are tainted and perverted by sin. Now, if we dare to deal with merits and entitlements, then what we must understand is that we must also include and attach demerits. If we then deal with demerits, that means that, when we are guilty of the very first infraction, retributive justice would have to say that we must die. For, the Bible says, "The soul that sinneth it shall die," and that

"The wages of sin is death." At this point, I then must raise an awesome question, and that question is, do we really want what we deserve? We are murmuring; we are bitter and resentful to God because we or others close to us didn't get what we felt like we or they were entitled to; we murmur that they deserve something better than they got, but I want us to retrospect for a moment. Go back over our lives for the last 10 years, well maybe last year, or maybe last month, or last week, or even the last few minutes and think about our sins and blemishes. Let's ask ourselves, do we really want what we deserve? How many of us would dare say to God, "God, give me what I really deserve"?

I just want to insert the fact that, no matter what infliction you have, it was infliction with a combination of restraining grace and tempered mercy, and at the worst, all we really get is severe visitation from God.

I don't know about you, but I don't want the Lord to give me what I deserve. I want Him to deal with me based on His grace because, even though I can't earn God's grace based upon my merits, neither can my demerits compel God to withdraw His grace. If I can't gain God's favor based on good works, neither can I lose His favor based on bad works. I don't know about you, but I've got some demerits. Maybe you don't have any demerits, but I've got some demerits. I've got some bad works, and I don't want God to deal with me on the basis of what I'm entitled to. I don't want God to give me what I really deserve, but I want Him to deal with me on the basis of grace.

When you look at the jealous murmurers, you will see that they did not grumble because of the fact that they received too little, but they grumbled because they were watching other workers, and they felt that the less-deserving workers were receiving the same amount as they were. The mistake that the 12-hour, murmuring workers made is the same mistake that we make. And that is, we engage in "split-posture vision." That is, with selfish envy and jealousy as the underlying factors, we have one eye on what God is doing for us and one eye on what God is doing for somebody else. This accounts for one reason we still have murmuring believers today. Our spirits are jaundiced, and our vision is split, and we wind up like the first workers. We prejudicially assess the fact that God has blessed those whom we believe to be the ill-deserving. And, instead of us rejoicing over God blessing others, we selfishly murmur and wind up charging God in a spirit of envy and jealousy with rank injustice. However, we must be careful about being envious, jealous, and coveting someone else's grace blessings because we don't know the price that they had to pay in order to receive them.

My friend, E. K. Bailey, told the story of a young minister who said to an old successful pastor, "I want to be just like you." The senior pastor replied, "You want to be just like me?" The young man said, "Yes sir, I want to be just like you." The old pastor said, "Let's pray." He said, "Lord, this young man said that he wants to be just like me. So Lord, let him get a church where the deacons and trustees will be mean. Let him get a church where the people will vote him out. Let him get a physical affliction in his body." At that moment, the young man interrupted the prayer and said, "Sir, I said I wanted to be just like you. I did not say that I wanted all of the trouble that you're praying about." The old pastor replied, "Son, if you want to be just like me, then you must go through the pains and the sufferings that I've gone through." We must be careful about being jealous and envious and coveting someone else's blessings because we don't know their hidden cross; we don't know the price that they had to pay.

To those of us believers who have split-posture vision and jaundiced spirits, there are some things that we see about God in this story. God, in His omniscience, knows that all of the workers, no matter when they are hired, are in desperate, dire need of His grace. He knows that we are all ill-deserving. Then, Kingdom remuneration belongs to God. God is sovereign and grace is sovereign. And, because grace is sovereign, God has the sovereign right to dispense His sovereign grace blessings as He pleases. God, in His beneficent benevolence, says in the Old Testament, "I will have mercy on whom I will have mercy." And then, in the text, God defends His uncalled-for generosity by asking a self-answering question, "Don't I have the right to do what I want with my own money?" And, because God is sovereign, not only does He have the right to bless and have mercy and bestow grace on whom He wills, He also does not owe anybody an explanation as to why He bestows His grace blessings as He does.

R. C. H. Lenski says, "There is no law or principle of right in heaven or earth forbidding the sovereign to exercise or bestow His grace." So, anyone who sees God through evil, envious eyes and charges Him with injustice and condemns grace insults God because God, being eternally free and omniscient, knows how to grant and bestow His sovereign grace without violating or compromising His untarnished justice or His unadulterated holiness. Instead of attacking God's sovereignty and His grace, and instead of watching God's dealings with others and comparing His dealings with us with how it appears that He is dealing with others, we ill-deserving grace recipients ought to take time to develop a grace attitude. And, when we develop a grace attitude, we will develop an attitude of gratitude for grace. And, with an attitude of gratitude, we won't have time for murmuring because our time will be consumed by thankfully counting our grace blessings. We will name them one by one. We will count our grace blessings, and we will see that God has given us much more than what we really could earn or even count.

And then finally, let's look at:

III. The Joyful Message

There is a hidden but implied message here. And, the hidden but implied message here is in between the lines. How do you suppose those eleventh hour, ill-deserving, called workers went home? If the 12-hour, hired workers were the only workers rebuked for murmuring, the opposite disposition is joy. So, the called workers went home joyfully. Now, the called, last workers didn't know about the uncalled-for generosity of the landowner, but though they didn't know about the uncalled-for generosity of the landowner, unlike the first workers who wanted a contract, the last workers trusted His goodness. And, because they trusted His goodness, they got His grace and His uncalled-for generosity and went home joyfully.

And, that's the message; don't worry about bargains and contracts with God. Just trust God's goodness and you will experience His grace and His uncalled-for generosity.

Now, the message is that none of us are 12-hour workers. All believers are, in a real sense, ill-deserving, eleventh hour workers. We are classified as eleventh hour workers because, like these workers, we were in desperate need, and our hope was eroding. We were in a paradoxical dilemma. And, the word *paradox* literally means "against the opinion." And, the fact is that a paradox is two truths that appear contradictory but are not. Look at our paradoxical dilemma:

We were dead and dying;

We were too mean to live, but not fit to die;

We were walking, talking dead men;

Too grand to waste, but too miserable to save;

Too dead to be alive, but too alive to be buried;

We were in the slave market of sin;

We had declared Chapter 7; and

We were totally and permanently bankrupt.

We were ill-deserving, unworthy, and inadequate. We were worms in the sense of being weak, worthless, and helpless. We had a debt that we could not pay. Romans 3 says, "We were unprofitable." That means something gone sour, and you throw away what has gone sour. We were living with the cataclysmic consequences of Adam's fall.

Just like the landowner came seeking those workers in desperate need, so God came to fallen man in desperate need. But, look at what God did; God came in the person of His Son Jesus to do us a grace favor. Jesus took our disgrace and shame upon Him and one Friday He died, was buried, and rose again.

The story is that there was an old woman who knew God well and totally trusted Him but had no money and no food in the house. So every day, she would go out on the porch and pray, "Lord, I need you to provide your child with some food." The old lady lived next door to an atheist, and one day, he got tired of hearing the old lady praying. So, he decided to shut her mouth. So, what he did was, he went to the store and bought a box of groceries and just laid them at her door. He left and watched for her to come out. When she came out to pray, she saw the groceries. So, she went to shouting, saying, "God, I thank you for providing." While she was shouting and thanking God, the atheist came over and told her, "Your God didn't provide that food, I bought that food." The woman got louder in her shout. The man said, "What are you shouting about now?" She said, "I'm shouting because this is the first time that I've seen how God provided the food and made an unbelieving fool like you pay the bill."

I'm here to tell us that, if we trust the goodness of God, we can experience God's grace and His uncalled-for generosity, and like the last workers and like this old lady, we can be joyful and shout. I don't know about you, but I have decided to trust the goodness of God, and I'm joyful and shouting because, at Calvary, God took care of my eternal needs. But now, every day, in grace, He takes care of my practical needs. Every time I turn around, I'm experiencing the Lord's grace and uncalled-for generosity. Instead of murmuring, I'm thanking God for His grace, His goodness, and His uncalled-for generosity. I'm joyful because He just keeps on generously meeting my needs.

I have an attitude of astonished, glad gratitude. The word *astonished* means "to be stung by a lick." And, the word *sting* means "to be pierced." So, I have been pierced by a lick of grace, and I'm glad about it. I have this attitude of astonished, glad gratitude because, even though I don't deserve it, God's grace just keeps blessings coming my way like ocean tidal waves. Before one tidal wave disappears, here comes another one. God gives me grace, and grace replaces grace. So, I'm joyful because God just keeps on generously meeting my needs.

Years ago, people used the expression, "say grace" for the prayer of thanksgiving at mealtime. There is the conviction that they said grace at mealtime, not because of the fact that they felt like they were entitled to the food, but they knew that their food was there by grace, and in reality, there was a dual emphasis. One, they knew that their food was the result of grace, and two, they would say "thank you" to God. In reality, they said grace as a means of saying thank you for grace. So, at mealtime, I'm like them; I say grace for God's grace. And, when I think about the fact that, by grace, "I am what I am," and by grace, God provides for my unworthiness and my inadequacies, all through the day in a spirit of joy, I can't help but "say grace."

I THOUGHT ON MY WAYS
Psalm 119:59

This is one of the most moving statements in all the psalms. It is one that should make us think seriously and soberly about our pursuits and conduct in life. If we would be honest with ourselves, we would confess that, in most cases, our ways are not pleasing to ourselves. There are some things about ourselves we don't like. There are some things about ourselves we wish were not there.

I have often said that, if we would be honest within and to ourselves, we would have to cry 'undone'; yet, to be honest with ourselves is hard to do. We like to tell ourselves that we are better than we know within ourselves we really are. It is hard for us to tell ourselves that wrong has the upper hand on us, and hence, we go on committing wrong and, at the same time, trying to pull the cover and hide our wrongs rather than meet face to face and eye to eye with our wrongs and confess them and turn to God with a repentant heart for forgiveness.

How easy is it for me to tell myself that my wrongs have been hidden? How easy it is for me to tell myself that my wrongs are all right as long as I don't do them in public. It is human to hide from the public, not considering the eyes of the public, knowing within ourselves that we are not what we want the public to think we are. We want the public to think we are angels. We put on our best front in public, hoping that our true selves will never be exposed. But even when our wrongs are hidden (as we think), there is an inner voice sounding within our conscience like distant thunder, telling us of our wrongs. Our conscience condemns us to ourselves, though we hate to admit it to ourselves and refuse to acknowledge our wrongs before God and repent.

We put on a self-righteous act in public, knowing that it is only an act; it is just an act, and that's all. But there are no isolated acts, and it is our acts that either justify us or condemn us. Our ways are the ways that make us. It is our ways that mold and shape us into having good or bad characters. It is easy to put on a hypocritical act. It is easy to pretend. It is easy to put on an outside show, but the time eventually comes when you must come face to face with the real you. When that time does come, you will be so proud of yourself.

The story is told of a man who had his picture painted with his face in his hands. The reason was to hide the scars on his face. The painting appeared as if he was in deep meditation. That was the impression he made in the public's eye. He wanted to appear saintly to the public, but though he tried ever so hard to hide his scars from the public, one day, he had to take his hands from his face, and the ugly scars remained to prove his unsaintliness. Rather, the scars revealed his reckless, riotous life in his youth.

Many people today are hiding their sinful ways from the public. Only, in time to come, they must be uncovered and disclosed. Covering up our sinful ways only lasts for a while, and then the cover is pulled from over them, and our true selves are exposed. Hiding from men is no justification for wrong, nor will it erase from memory a guilty conscience.

The Bible paints men just as they are inside. The Bible writes men's record by what they actually do and not by what they say and pretend to be. We try to hide from men and fool the public. We try to look good on the outside; we put on and show off. We try to impress the public with our goodness, even with hate and jealousy in our hearts. We grin in the face of the public with the shame of our sins open before the eyes of God.

We seek public opinion rather than divine approval. What the public thinks and sanctions is what we label as being the thing to do (right or wrong), but what the public thinks and labels as being right is not always, and very seldom is right in the eyes of God. It is not what men think that makes the difference. It is what God says in His Word.

Never can we measure our righteousness by men or according to human standards. The highest human standard is too low for God. In His Word, He has set up a standard by which men are to live, and any deviation from the standard means a clash with His divine will and trouble in the life of the offender.

Many are the human wrecks that clashed with God's divine will and plan for their lives, such as the hardhearted sinner, the unbelieving atheist and infidel, the skeptical agnostic, the criminal in prison, and the drunkard in the gutter.

The same is true of the prodigal son in the hog pen, the prostitute on the corner, the incorrigible boy and girl at home, the murderer on death row, the hardened criminal fleeing from justice, the dope pusher on the school campus, and the dope addict with a warped mind.

The same is the case of the homosexual dying with AIDS, the dope users in mental institutions in padded cells, the young dropouts of home, church, and school who roam the street and alleys; the pimp who uses once virtuous girls to make a living for him by selling their bodies, the mother who gives her child away like an unwanted puppy, and the gambler who loses his hard earned money and lets his family go hungry, naked, and cold.

So it is with the swindler who takes advantage of others in order to survive, the father or mother who commits incest with his/her children, and the youth with broken health by riotous living.

All of these and millions more have clashed with God's plan for their lives, and the wreck, shame, heartbreak, agony, and death that they experienced is more than pitiful. There is no way to beat the law of retribution. What you sow, you shall reap. What you put out will come back to you. If you dig a ditch for a brother, dig two, for the first one is yours.

To go headlong against God and His Word means that you are headed for a sudden or eventual fall. Your choice of conduct must be decisive. You choose either the good or the bad. You choose either the right or the wrong. You choose either the best or the worst. You choose either to obey or disobey. You choose either to live life on a high plain or live in the gutter with disgrace and shame. You choose either to walk the straight and narrow path in peace or to walk the broad road to death and an untimely grave. You choose either to be a man or a puppet. You choose either to be somebody or a straggler. You choose either to be a blessing to the world or a disgrace to society. You choose either to be a real woman or a strumpet on the streets.

The power of thought is a great privilege, being endowed by our Creator; therefore, it is this power that determines what we do—good or bad, right or wrong. If man thinks straight, he will go straight. If he thinks wrong, he will act wrong. If he aims high, he will aim for the heights. If he thinks wholesome thoughts, he will do noble deeds. If he thinks low, he will stoop to low things. Our thoughts go before our actions.

Martin Luther once said, "I can't keep birds from flying over my head, but I can keep them from building a nest under my hat."

We cannot keep temptations from coming our way, but we can keep from being entangled by them. We are not responsible for temptations coming to our door, but we are responsible for allowing them to enter by our idleness, slothfulness, wastefulness, recklessness, riotousness, and debauchery, which lead to eternal ruin. Temptation will come. Satan is good at enticing and camouflaging. He's a master at trickery and knows how to fool you. He knows how to get your attention. He knows your human weakness. He knows your soft spots. He knows the tender places. He knows what we like and what we don't like. He knows what to tempt us with and what not to tempt us with.

Therefore, he never comes with something that he knows you don't like, and if he does bring something you don't like, he brings it with the intention of making you like it. Unless one has his/her thinking cap on and is thinking straight, he/she is a prime target for Satan.

Nobody who thinks straight wants to be in prison. Nobody who thinks straight wants to be broken down in health as the result of riotous living. Nobody who thinks straight wants to be in an asylum. Nobody who thinks straight wants to spend the rest of their days in a rest home because of reckless, riotous living. Nobody in their right mind wants to be cut all to pieces or shot down like a street dog for playing bad, and nobody wants to live with human blood dripping from their murderous hands and the memory haunting their conscience night and day, having slain someone out of foolishness.

It takes a lot of straight thinking to live soberly and sanely in this present day society. All of the wildness, recklessness and murder we are witnessing among our young people today is because they won't think straight. This is a generation of know-all among our youth. They feel that they know more at thirteen or fifteen than we older people know at fifty or seventy.

All of the suicides and suicide attempts by teenagers and young adults are caused because they don't think. They thought that suicide was the best way out. They thought that, by committing suicide, they would get away from it all. But in committing suicide, you don't get away at all. There is a judgment day coming, and what will your answer be at the judgment bar of God?

Solomon was right when he said that "the way of transgressors is hard . . . There is a way which seemeth right unto a man, but the end thereof are the ways of death." Jesus said, "Broad is the way, that leadeth to destruction, and many there be which go in thereat: Because strait is the gate, and narrow is the way, which leadeth unto life, and few there be that find it." The Lord honors the way of the upright but frowns upon the way of the ungodly and unthoughtful. Unthoughtful men always end up in trouble with God.

The Bible, history, and the book of observation are quite replete with sad stories of men and women and young people who failed to think seriously and sanely about life and the consequences of sinful and unthoughtful ways in life. Read the sad story of the tragic end of Ahab and his idolatrous wife, Jezebel. Ahab died in the garden of Jezreel at the hand of Jehu, and Jezebel was trampled to death by the feet of war-horses, and the dogs of the streets licked her blood and devoured her vile body.

Please remember the two sons of Eli, the priest, who died at the edge of the sword in the hand of their enemies because they honored not God and committed fornication in the house of God. Don't forget about Eli who failed to correct them and condemn them for their licentious act.

The list is long of those who ignored God and His Word and ended up in the gaul of bitterness. Listen to the chronicle which the Word of God provides.

Cain with his murderous hands.

Saul with his evil eyes.

Absalom with his rebellious spirit.

The seven sons of Saul hanging dead from trees.

Gehazi covered with the leprosy of Naaman because of his greed.

Forty-two children eaten by bears from the wilderness because they mocked the prophet Elisha.

The destruction of the posterity of Ahab by Jehu because of the wickedness of the mother and father.

Jeroboam who did evil in the sight of the Lord.

Nebuchadnezzar and Belshazzar with their ungodly, haughty spirits.

Zachariah and Hosea who also did evil in the sight of God.

Judas Iscariot who committed suicide for betraying his Lord and many others.

But lest we forget, let's remember the suffering of King David for his murderous act of having his servant Uriah killed in order to take his wife, Bathsheba.

Men may do their dirt, but underneath that dirt is an unseen hand that uncovers it. Men may try to run away from their crimes, but I tell you, there is nowhere neither to run nor hide. The ghost of a man's deeds follows him wherever he goes.

A man may commit a crime and run away from the law, but he can never outrun his deeds. Cain tried that after killing his brother Abel, but wherever he went, the blood of his brother was ever before his eyes, and his dying groans pierced his ears. Paul says that he that doeth wrong shall receive the wrong which he hath done. When a man's ways pleases the Lord, He makes his enemies be at peace with him. But when a man's ways displeases the Lord, enemies defeat him.

Royal robes, glittering crowns, loyal servants, royal thrones, royal scepters, signet rings, and royal palaces do not interest God, nor do they ward off justice. He that soweth to the flesh shall of the flesh reap corruption. He who defrauds his brother will be defrauded by a brother. Not only are we punished for our sins, but, often, the punishment assumes the form of the sins that we have committed. Jacob deceived his brother Esau and lived to see himself being cruelly deceived by his own sons.

There is only one way to get the sin problem and the guilty conscience solved and dissolved, and that way is by thinking on our ways and repenting of our sins and turning to God for forgiveness.

Our way is not God's way. Our way is an offense to God. Our way is an insult to God. Our way is a stench in the nostrils of God. Our way is in defiance of God and is contrary to the will of God.

Our way is insubordination to the Law of God. Our way is rebellion against God. Our way is displeasing to God. Our way grieves the heart of God. Our way dishonors God. Our way is disobedience to God. Our way is ingratitude to God. Our way is an attempt to discredit God. Our way expresses disbelief in God. Our way makes us spurn the grace of God. Our way robs us of fellowship with God. Our way leads us away from God. Our way makes us feel we have no need of God and hardens our hearts toward God.

Our way brings grief, sorrow, bitter tears of regret, and misery. Our way brings suffering, trouble, woe, heartbreak, and scars. Our way brings shame, disgrace, poverty, and leads to the gutter.

Our way leads to rottenness and ruin. Our way is dangerous, rough, degenerated, demoralizing, and degrading. Our way is hard, perverse, unholy, defiled, and impure.

Our way leads to leanness of soul, emptiness of life, hardness of heart, and leads down a dark path in life. Our way leads to a wasted life, a wretched life, an unprofitable life, an unhappy life, a fruitless life, and a joyless life. Our way leads to a warped mind, a poisoned system, a human wreck, licentiousness, and prodigality. Our way leads to murder, to self-murder, to a broken home and to an early grave under condemnation and judgment of God.

But God's way leads to life here, peace of mind, happiness, joy, salvation, justification, sanctification, spiritual adoption, and pureness of heart.

God's way leads to wholeness of the whole man, makes us new creatures in Christ Jesus, members of the royal family, and makes us heir to all that heaven has. God's way makes life worthwhile, fruitful, relieves the guilty conscience, and redeems lost souls.

God's way is light on a dark path, a lamp unto our feet, and directs our footsteps. God's way is the way to seek. God's way is the true way, the sure way, the safe way, the right way, the good way, the best way, and the way to follow.

God's way is the way in, the way out, the way over, the way under, the way across, the way in life, the way for life, the holy way, the righteous way, and the blessed way. God's way is the sacred way, the straight way, the narrow way, and the only way.

Paul writes, "Finally brethren, whatsoever things are true, whatsoever things are honest, whatsoever things are just, whatsoever things are pure, whatsoever things are lovely, whatsoever things are of good report, think on these things."

I plead with you today to think on your ways and turn your feet unto the Lord's testimonies. Keep your mind stayed on Jesus, and let His Word be your daily guide. The Law of the Lord is perfect, converting the soul. The testimony of the Lord is sure, making wise the simple. The statutes of the Lord are right, rejoicing the heart. The commandment of the Lord is pure, enlightening the eyes. The fear of the Lord is clean, enduring forever. The judgments of the Lord are true and righteous altogether; more are they to be desired than gold, yea! than much fine gold; they are sweeter than honey and the honeycomb. Moreover, by them is thy servant warned and in keeping of them there is great reward. Think on your ways and turn to God now. He waits with outstretched arms, waiting patiently for your return.

I WAS GLAD WHEN THEY SAID UNTO ME: LET US GO INTO THE HOUSE OF THE LORD
Psalm 122:1

The one hundred and twenty-second psalm, and especially the first verse, is quite familiar, especially to churchgoers of every faith.

It holds first place as being one of the favorites, both throughout Judaism and the Christian world. Somehow, it seems to lodge in the hearts, hinge upon the tongues, and rest upon the minds of churchgoing people the world over.

Although it was written and sung antiphonally when Israel was called to worship on the Sabbath day, it was expressed in action many centuries before when Cain and Abel built their crude altar and worshiped before the Lord.

The words of the text express the greatest joy to be found by God-fearing, God-loving, and churchgoing people. To frequently go to the house of God for worship is innate in the born-again soul. Christian fellowship with the saints is inescapable in the Christian experience. We feel that we just have to go to church. If we can't go anywhere else, for God's sake, let us go to church.

Even though we are hindered from going sometimes by circumstances over which we have no control, there is a desire, a yearning, and a longing to be there. If you take the church away from us, our lives would be empty and miserable. Private and family devotions hold a special place in the moral and spiritual development of believers, but they do not take the place of public worship in the house of God in fellowship with the saints.

Oliver Wendell Holmes once said, "I find that amid my busy everyday affairs that there is deeply embedded in me, in the corner of my heart, a little plant called reverence that wants to be watered at least once a week." Like Mr. Holmes, I find that, deep down on the inside of me, there is something called the soul that gets hungry and thirsty for the Word of God and communion with the saints sometimes even before the week ends. Nothing will satisfy that longing, that hunger, and that thirst but the prayers of the saints, the songs of Zion, a message from God's Word, and the fellowship and hand shakes with others.

I break off here to say that the message must come from the Word of God. I don't want to go to church on Sunday morning and hear no word from the Lord. I don't want to go to church on Sunday morning and hear a political address. I don't like a lot of program on Sunday morning, no matter how good it is. I don't want to hear a speech, no matter how good it is, and I don't want a speech, no matter who delivers it.

When I go to church on Sunday morning, I just want church, good church, live church, with sincerity in worship. There is something in public worship that reaches deep into the innermost being like nothing else is able to reach. The individual peculiarity is toned down when sincere prayers are uttered and the singing is alive and when the preacher is on fire. The testimonies of the saints concerning the goodness of God inspire others to hold on, even when life seems to be tumbling in on them.

In public worship, the blessings of God are recalled, and thanksgiving for even a little is prayed for by those with grateful hearts. The giving of tithes and offerings is done with a spirit of gratitude and reverence, while the bread and wine draw our hearts and minds to Calvary as we observe the Lord's death.

In public worship, in the house of God, the children of God feel a spiritual kinship. There, we share our mutual woes, bear our mutual burdens, and often shed for each a sympathizing tear. In worship in the house of God, perplexing problems of everyday life are forgotten for a while.

In public worship, the sorrows of the heart are often softened and soothed, and the loads of life become lighter. The storms of life are quelled for a season. In the house of God, we feel a sense of security. In the house of God, we are made to know that somebody cares. Somehow, we catch a glimpse of a ray of hope in the midst of despair. In the house of God, we find listening ears and understanding hearts. In the house of God, lonely hearts find comfort, and those who have been battered and bruised all week long find healing balm for their wounds. In the house of God, the outcast finds a shelter, the stranger finds himself among friends, and the traveler finds strength for his journey. Prodigals are restored to the Father's house, and the lost man finds his way to life by the light of the cross. In the house of God, little children learn that God is a loving Father and that Jesus is their friend. In the house of God, weak Christians gain strength, and strong Christians are made stronger.

The reading and hearing of God's Word makes us determined to put on the whole armor of God and to press forward toward the mark for the prize of the high calling which is in Christ Jesus. The reading and hearing of God's Word causes us to look for His glorious appearing in the clouds in glorious majesty to judge the quick and the dead and to change our vile bodies and make them like unto His glorious body according to the mighty working and infinite knowledge and omnipotent power whereby He promises to subdue all things unto Himself.

There is a spiritual ear in every Christian's heart that gives meaning to the words of the psalmist as he wrote, "Deep calleth unto deep." The depth of the human soul calls to the depths of divine mercy. This is the cry of the Christian heart, not justice but mercy. The psalmist knew by personal experience that nothing was more profitable to him than a seat in the tabernacle with the rest of God's people for true and sincere worship on the Sabbath day. Thus he said, "I had rather be a doorkeeper in the house of God, than to dwell in the tents of wickedness ... My soul longeth, yea even, fainteth for the carts of the Lord." Thus he cried in the ears of Israel, "O come, let us worship and bow down: let us kneel before the Lord our maker ... O magnify the Lord with me, and let us exalt his name together ... Make a joyful noise unto the Lord."

David, the king, did not allow thrones, scepters, crowns, royal robes, and subjects to eclipse his vision of God nor make him forsake regular worship on the Sabbath day. He gave God top priority in his everyday affairs and made the worship services his weekly delight. He gave God credit for all he accomplished, be it provinces, subjects, or rulership for sheep. He took no credit to himself but gave all praise and glory to God. I can almost hear him saying now, "I will lift up my eyes unto the hills from whence cometh my help. My help cometh from the Lord, who made heaven and earth."

"One thing have I desired of the Lord, that will I seek after; that I may dwell in the house of the Lord all the days of my life, to behold the beauty of the Lord, and to enquire in his temple."

It disturbs me when I see Christians who are careless about going to church. It bothers me to no end when I see church members more concerned about taverns than they are about the house of God. It upsets me to see church members who are so impatient in church and so relaxed anywhere else. In the house of God, His glory can be seen. In the house of God, His presence can be felt. It is there that the Holy Spirit makes His abode. It is in the house of God that His presence among God's people is manifested. The Gospel that I hear in the house of God is food for my hungry soul.

It puzzles me and really upsets me when I see so many church members with all their freedom, conveniences, good health, working on good jobs, wearing fine clothes, living in fine houses, and yet do not have time for God or His Church. It bothers me to no end when I see church members (if they come to church at all) drag in. They come late and leave early. They live in fine houses that God has given them, dress in fine clothes, get in twenty thousand dollar cars, and drive across town late to give God a dollar and get insulted if the church asks them for more.

The church really means nothing to them as long as they are up, but they cry to God and beg the church when sickness strikes and trouble rises. They cry out to God if their family is about to be broken up or if their children break their hearts because they are incorrigible and face a prison sentence or are killed in cold blood. When they face a foreclosure or find themselves unable to pay the rent, gas, and light bills, it is then that they can find the preacher, whom they declared they did not want to hear. It is then that they can find the church and ask for help, even though they have walked by it day after day when things were going well.

Allow me to interject here. Those of you who are negligent, slothful, and careless about going to church, you need to spur up because the time will come when you must bow before Him. The time will come when you are going to need an earnest prayer on your behalf. The time will come when you will call some minister, even if it is only for a funeral. The time will come when you will need the church songs to be sung over your lifeless remains. The time will come when the Bible will be read whether at your sickbed or at your graveside. The time will come when some church preacher is going to have to commit your body to the ground, ashes to ashes and dust to dust.

So, I say today, why not go while you can? Why wait until life tumbles in on you? Why wait until you are helpless or on a sickbed? Why wait until trouble strikes? Why wait until death knocks at your door? Why wait until the doctor says he can do you no good? Why wait until God makes His move against you? When God makes His move, you are through. When God makes His move, friends are of no help. When God makes His move, doctors are of no value.

When God makes His move, dearest loved ones stand helpless. When God makes His move, the strongest medicine is impotent. When God makes His move, hospitals are powerless. When God makes His move, mother nor father, brother nor sister can help. When God makes His move, pleading for mercy is too late. When God makes His move, tears of regret will mean nothing. When God makes His move, prayer for more time and another opportunity will be denied. When God makes His move, excuses for your neglect will not be honored. When God makes His move, no proxy is accepted. When God makes His move, time wasters, haughty spirits, and procrastinators are humbled. When God makes His move, hard hearts are softened. When God makes His move, high heads bow. When God makes His move, those who refuse to go to church wish they had gone. When God makes His move, idle hands are paralyzed.

Every church member ought to make it a must to go to church as often as he or she can. It is not enough to join the church just to have your name on the church roll. To go to church is a privilege and a Christian's duty. It is not only a privilege and duty, but for born-again folks, it is a joy. One does not know how much he or she needs the church until he or she has need for it.

I go to church because I need to go.
I go to church because I ought to go.
I go to church because I know I should go.
I go to church because something in me compels me to go.
I go to church because I have to go.
I go to church because I must go.
I go to church because I love to go.
I go to church because it is my duty to go.
I go to church because it is a privilege to go.
I go because I get joy out of going.
I go because I am ever in need of spiritual help.
I go because I need spiritual strength.
I go because I need spiritual guidance.

I go because it is right to go.
I go to be spiritually enlightened.
I go to be spiritually indoctrinated.
I go that I might be fed with the Word.
I go that I might get a spiritual lift.
I go that I might be reminded of my human shortcomings.
I go that the preacher might chastise me, for my wrongdoings.
I go because I need the Gospel message to condemn me for my sins.
I go because I need the preacher to show me God's way for my footsteps.
I go because I need the Word of God preached Sunday after Sunday to
    me that I might know what the will of the Lord is for my life.
I go that I might know better how to live life as a Christian.

I go to church for spiritual nourishment.
I go to church that the preacher might show me my true self.
I go for my own soul's benefit.
I go to church to be moved on the inside.

I go to meet my brothers and sisters in Christ.
I go to church to be prayed for.
I go to pray for others.
I go to join in the singing.

I go because the Lord is there to forgive me of my sins when I confess.
I go because the Lord is there to bless my soul.
I go to learn about God's works and ways.
I go to learn more about the Bible.
I go for Christian fellowship.
I go to testify to the goodness of God.
I go to witness to the truth of the Gospel.
I go because I am saved by the blood of the cross.

I go because I love the Lord.
I go because I love the church.
I go in the heat, and I go in the cold.
I go in the sunshine, and I go in the rain.
I go in the daytime, and I go in the night.
I go to church to mingle my voice with the saints.
I go to church for a spiritual feast on bread and wine at the Lord's table.

I tell you, take the church away from me, and life for me would be empty. The church is the source of all my earthly joys. Like the psalmist, I am glad when it is time to go to church. The church house walls seem to beckon me. The church house doors swing open to welcome me. In the church house, I stand in awe before the Holy and righteous God. I view an old rugged cross on which my Savior died. By faith, I can see blood dripping from my Master's side, like surging water in an overflowing stream. I am made conscious of the fact that, in His death, He redeemed and saved me; looking beyond my human faults, He saw my needs. Why then wouldn't I love and go to His church? Christians ought to be glad when it is time for them to go to church. I am always glad when it is church time.

I know the church has some weak members, but let me go to it. I know it has some stumbling, blundering, falling, and failing members, but let me go to it. I know that some of the members have ugly ways, but let me go to church.

I know that the church has some disgruntled members, but let me go to it. I know that the church has false pretenders and hypocrites in it, but let me go to it. I know that the church has some troublemakers, but let me go to it. I know that the church has some traitors in it, but let me go to it. I know that the church has some peace breakers and church disturbers in it, but let me go to it. I know there are deceitful members there, but I just have to go.

I know that some members are halfhearted, cold, and indifferent, but let me go to church. I know there are some loose livers there, but I just have to go. I know there are some mean folks in the church, but let me go to church. I know that there are false accusers there, but let me go just the same.

I know the church has some drinking members in it, but let me go. I know the church does not have one member who is absolutely perfect. Neither am I, but to refuse to go on that account, I can't do it.

Going to church is my life. Going to church is the source of all my joys. The ancient Hebrews seemed to have had high respect and great reverence for worship. They had a perfect knowledge of what it meant to assemble themselves together to praise God. To worship God at crude altars and in the tabernacle before the Temple was built was important to them.

Abraham, the friend of God, on his long journey at the order of God to leave Ur of the Chaldeans to go to Canaan, stopped on his way and built an altar unto God and worshiped. Jacob took the stone on which he slept the night he fled from his brother Esau on his way to Padan-aram and used it for his altar and worshiped God; he named the place Bethel, saying, "The Lord is in this place, and this stone that I have set for a pillar shall surely be the Lord's house."

From the Scriptures, we observe that God accepts and sanctifies the places of worship dedicated to Him. He hallows the spot of ground on which they sit and renders sacred every piece of material which goes into their construction, be it a crude altar or a magnificent temple. He had as much respect for Abraham's crude altar as he did for David's tabernacle. He had as much respect for Jacob's stone at Bethel as He did for Solomon's Temple in Jerusalem. And He is present wherever two or three are gathered together in His name as much as He is when a multitude comes together.

God is so concerned about places of worship and the worshippers. When ordering Moses to build the tabernacle in the wilderness, He drew for him the blue print and chose the spot of ground where the tabernacle should rest. He selected the kind and quality of the material that went into it from the outer court to the inner court and from the gate to the most holy place where the Ark of the Covenant did rest. He designed the Ark of the Covenant Himself, sanctified and hallowed it, having already thundered His laws from Mt. Sinai, which were contained in the Ark. He selected the quality and colors of the curtains which veiled the Holy of Holies, where Aaron and the other priests in the exercise of their sacerdotal functions ministered behind mystical curtains upon smoking altars, offering sacrifices to God and making intercession for the people.

The attire of the high priest included his robe, his Ephod, the Urim, and the Thumim, which God designed. After the completion of the tabernacle, God chose to sit above the mercy seat, over the Ark of the Covenant, between the two cherubs whose wings of gold touched each other at the center.

The hallowed tabernacle was entered with awe and reverential fear. The worshippers were conscious of God's presence in the tabernacle and of the awesomeness of His presence. Therefore, on Friday, the adults and children made ready to meet the Lord in the tabernacle on Saturday, although it was built portable. They got ready to go to church. They didn't come to church just any old way, nor did they come just any old time. You see, it is the worshippers who make the day a day of worship.

Solomon's magnificent Temple would have been a waste of time and money and hard labor if it had not been for the worshipers who assembled in it for worship. However, worship in any place must be out of our love for God. We may go to church every Sunday in the year and not worship because we have no love for God or for His church. If God is not the center of our worship, we have only a gathering of people together on Sunday. God and His Church must be the center of Christian worship.

All adoration and praise must be to the Eternal.
All form and fashion must be laid aside.
All petty jealousy must be eliminated.
All selfishness must be forsaken.
All malice must be put out of mind.
All hatred must be banished from the heart.
All wrong done to us must be forgiven.
All sin must be confessed and repentance acknowledged.

There is no worship where there is hatred, bitterness, and strife. There is no worship where there is insincerity. When it comes to worship, we have to get down to business. God must be seen in the light of His holiness. Cathedrals and magnificent temples and beautifully designed modern church houses are meaningless if the glory of God cannot be seen by the worshipers who assemble in them.

The ancient Hebrews had great reverence for God and the sanctity of His house. Even today, the temples and synagogues are entered with reverence and thanksgiving. They, like the ancients, consider their synagogues and temples to be the places where God's glory is seen and where His honor dwells. It is the place where they take sweet communion, both with God and with each other, seated upon a common footstool of mercy.

The thing that seemed to disturb Israel the most when they were in captivity in Babylon was being deprived of the privilege of worshiping God in the Temple in Jerusalem. If you could go to Jerusalem today, you would see hundreds of Jews at the Wailing Wall, weeping and wailing and almost going into a frenzy in a prayer of repentance, yearning to become worthy to worship in the Temple. In Babylonian captivity, they yearned for the day when they could go back home to worship God like they did in former days.

Thus, they cried, "If I forget Thee O Jerusalem, let my right hand forget her cunning. If I do not remember Thee, let my tongue cleave to the roof of my mouth. If I prefer not Jerusalem above my chief joy, let me lose the use of my right arm." For "the Lord loveth the gates of Zion more than all the dwellings of Jacob." Even though in Babylonian captivity they sang, "I will lift up mine eyes unto the hills, from whence cometh my help." My help cometh, not from the Babylonian King; "My help cometh from the Lord, which made heaven and earth."

"I will bless the Lord at all times: his praise shall continually be in my mouth." When they returned from captivity and approached their homeland, their eyes were fastened on the Temple in Jerusalem. Solomon built the Temple in Jerusalem with so much architectural skill that neither a hammer nor saw was heard ringing from its roof nor walls.

He contracted with Hiram, king of Tyre, for timber, both fir and cedar hewn from Mt. Lebanon. He sent 50,000 men to bear burdens, and he sent 3,600 men to supervise the work. He contracted with Hiram, the widow's son, who made vases of emerald and gold and silver. He made doorknobs and hinges of brass. He made artificial flowers of gold and, according to legend, the flowers looked so real that the bees swarmed about them, seeking nectar.

He made doorposts of cedar and overlaid them with pure gold. He made candlesticks of brass and snuff dishes of brass. He overlaid the beams, the posts, and the lintels with gold and engraved cherubims upon the walls. He made two cherubims of pure gold which he placed above the Ark of the Covenant, whose wings touched each other at the center. He made the veil of the Temple of blue and purple and crimson and fine linen. He made an altar of brass in the Holy of Holies in which the priest entered once a year to offer sacrifices for the people.

Around the Temple, he made a molten sea and upon the walls around about, He carved and placed oxen made of gold, 12 in number; three looking east, three looking west, three looking north, and three looking south. He made chains of gold and artificial pomegranates. He made ten lavers of brass and chains of gold. He made 100 basins of gold and shovels made of brass. He made ten tables and placed five on each side of the altar in the Temple.

The lights in the Temple burned brightly from the seven branch lamp stands made of brass. He made spoons and vessels for the Lord's house, the cost of which by weight cannot be measured.

They called it the Temple of the Lord, the Temple of God, the holy Temple, the house of the Lord, the house of God, and the Father's house. They called it the house of prayer, the house of God's glory, the house of sacrifice, the house of their sanctuary, the holy and beautiful house, and holy Mt. Zion. They called it the mountain of the Lord's house, the place where God's honor dwells, the tabernacle of witness, and the joy of the whole earth.

To this magnificent temple came Jewish worshipers once a year from every quarter. But they, like so many of us, turned from God and began to worship idols after the death of Solomon. One day, they found themselves captives being carried into Babylon under the mighty and ruthless army of Nebuchadnezzar, king of Babylon.

Servitude and mockery by the Babylonians was all they could expect. Their mockers would often say to them, "Sing us one of the songs of Zion." Their only answer was, "How can we sing the Lord's songs in a strange and godless land?" Again, I say to church members, you don't know how bad you need the church till you have need of it. But though we drag and often play church, God will never be left without a witness.

These would-be-pious Jews were so dejected by their own doings and idolatry that, in captivity, they wanted to sing but could not sing. They wanted to play their harps but couldn't play. They simply hung their harps on the willow trees, sat down, and wept when they remembered the day they had their freedom to worship God as they wanted to but went the way of least resistance.

But I say once again, people ought to serve God while they have the chance. They ought to pray while they are on their feet. We might feel that we are doing God a favor by our coming to church, but our coming to church adds nothing to God, nor is He excited about our coming. It is a blessing and a privilege for us to go to church. If all the preachers of the earth should decide to stop preaching; if all of the singers should decide to stop, leave the choir stands, and sing no more; if all the church members should decide to stop going to church and worship God no more; and if every church door should close and call the worshipers together no more, God would not be without witness.

The psalmist writes, "The heavens declare the glory of God, the firmaments showeth His handiwork. Day after day uttereth speech and night unto night showeth forth knowledge." Though nature be hushed and quiet, when the sun in its glory has reached its zenith on the azure blue vaulted sky; though the world keep her silent festivals when the stars shine brightest at night, the psalmist says they speak of God's glory, majesty, and power, declaring Him worthy of praise.

One day takes up the story of telling the world of God's greatness, while the preceding days told the same story. Jesus said that, If we should hold our peace, rocks will cry out in praise to the King Eternal.

Jesus himself found it necessary and beneficial to go to church. He called it His Father's house and House of Prayer. He was zealous about keeping it sacred and declared its sanctity. He defended its holiness, and upheld its laws. He stood by its principles, sang with the congregation, read the Scriptures when asked to do so, and He bowed in prayer with the rest of the worshipers. He cherished the sacred ground where the synagogue rested, and He entered the Temple with reverence. He helped the poor who lay at the Temple gate and asked for alms. He declared His mission in the world at church as He read the prophecy of Isaiah concerning His coming to earth.

If Jesus found it profitable and even demanded of Himself to go to church, why can't we be glad when it is church time? I am always glad to go to church. I don't need any coaxing and coercing, nor do I need any prodding. Nobody has to fuss at me about going because I am always glad when Sunday comes. I delight to be with my brothers and sisters, and I am always glad to behold their smiles. I look forward to a handshake, and I love to join in the singing. I love to hear the saints pray for me and others. I love to hear the Scriptures being read. I rejoice to hear others testify about the goodness of God.

Though it shakes me up and sometimes condemns me, I love to hear the preacher preach the gospel unafraid and unashamed. I don't have to be on program, just let me be there. Just let me ease into the sanctuary and sit among the children of God, and I am all right.

His presence can be felt. The Holy Spirit takes over when hearts are right. The fellowship of Christians is beyond comparison. There is a sweet communion there. The kindest sympathies are extended, and the most lasting friendships are formed. The strongest ties of love bind us together, and there is a mutual understanding among believers.

There is something in worship that satisfies me. There is something there that makes my heart rejoice. The worship service makes me forget my troubles, lifts my heavy load, and brightens my day. I see Christ in the beauty of His holiness. I hear from heaven through God's Word. My hopes are inspired, my faith made stronger, and I get a glimpse of the glories of heaven. I am glad to go to church. I have to go to church. About all I know is church. I know very little about the world outside. I was begotten by a church father, and I was conceived by a church mother. I was born into a church home and reared in a church environment. I was told that, when I was a baby, my mother carried me to church. My first school days were in a church house. I was taught my first little prayer, "Now I lay me down to sleep" on my church mother's knee. The first song I ever learned was a church song, "Bye and Bye."

When my mother and father died, church folks took an interest in me. When my grandfather died, my two sisters, Julia and Leora, who were church members, took me in and did what they could for me, keeping before me an abiding faith in God and His church. When I was ten years old, I was converted by the Reverend A. D. Barker and, on the first Sunday in September, I was baptized into the church in the Arkansas River.

The little education I have, I received by attending church-related schools. Whatever my accomplishments are, I have gained by my association and affiliation with church institutions. When I married, I married a church girl. We have striven to rear five church children who are a blessing to us and the Christian world. All of my grandchildren are church grandchildren. When I die, I want to be buried by the church. I want church songs sung over my body, and I want the Bible, the church's book, to be read. I want my obituary to reflect my church life. I want a church preacher to preach my funeral. I want my body carried to the cemetery by church members. I want a church preacher to commit my body to the ground, ashes to ashes and dust to dust.

So, I say to you, come on and go with me to church. Let us join in the worship with the saints of God. "O magnify the Lord with me, and let us exalt His name together. Worship the Lord with gladness, come before His presence with thanksgiving, enter into His courts with praise. Make a joyful noise unto the Lord and bless His Holy name. O come, let us worship and bow down, Let us kneel before the Lord our Maker, be thankful unto Him and bless His name. Praise the Lord in His sanctuary. Give thanks in the great congregation. Give unto the Lord the glory due His name. Make a joyful noise unto Him, all ye lands. Serve the Lord with gladness. Come before His presence with singing.

"The Lord hath done great things for us, whereof we ought to be glad."

THE IMMUTABILITY OF CHRIST

Hebrews 13:8

Among the many great fundamental doctrines set forth in the Bible is the doctrine of the immutability of Christ. The word "immutability" simply means changelessness, not subject to change, eternal stability, or unchangeable.

Although the word "immutable" appears only twice, and the word "immutability" appears only once in the Bible, Hebrews 6:17-18 and 13:8 are passages in the Bible which throw floodlights upon the truth of this great and all important doctrine.

In the prophecy of Malachi, chapter 3, verse 6, the Master speaks Himself saying, "I am the Lord, I change not." In the epistle of James, chapter 1, verse 17, it is written, "With [Him] is no variableness, neither shadow of turning." In Psalm 102:25-27, we read, "Of old hast thou laid the foundation of the earth: and the heavens are the work of thy hands. They shall perish, but thou shalt endure: yea, all of them shall wax old as a garment; as a vesture shalt thou change them ... But thou art the same, and thy years shall have no end."

In the Book of Jude, this solemn benediction is given; "to the only wise God our Savior, the Lord Jesus Christ be glory and honor, dominion and power, both now and forever. Amen." In 1 Timothy 6:15-16, Paul calls Him "the blessed and only Potentate, the King of kings and Lord of lords, who only hath immortality." In the Book of Exodus, we learn that Jesus Christ of Nazareth is the same great I AM of eternity, speaking to Moses from the burning bush at the foot of a mount called Horeb.

The model prayer set forth by Jesus in both Matthew and Luke closes with these words, "For thine is the kingdom and the power and glory, forever and ever, Amen." In the text, the writer of the Book of Hebrews says, "Jesus Christ, the same yesterday, today and forever." To us, yesterday is too far back for us, and forever is too far ahead of us to comprehend it, and today is too uncertain; but Jesus Christ is the same in eternity, in time, and in the future.

While the writer of the text uses the word "same" as an adjective, with reference to the immutability or changelessness of Christ, the ancient religious mystics used it as a noun when referring to the all-wise, eternal God. They called Him "the same." They revered Him as "the same." They honored Him as "the same." They worshiped Him as "the same." They prayed to Him as "the same," and they took refuge in Him whom they knew as being "the same."

This is exactly what the writer of the text meant when saying that Jesus Christ is the same yesterday, today, and forever. The adjective used by the writer of the text setting forth the doctrine of the immutability of Jesus Christ does not destroy the noun used in calling Him the same by the mystics, nor does the noun "same" destroy the beauty of the adjective which the writer of the text uses in his writing.

Christ is both the noun "same" and the adjective used by the writer, the same yesterday and today and forever. He is both the noun "same" and the adjective "same" in His divine person. Being the great God that He is, He must be eternally the same and remain eternally the same. Christ cannot be anything less than immutable because it is essential to His eternity of being. It is one of the incommunicable attributes or one of the foundation stones upon whom His deity must rest.

Deity includes immutability; therefore, Christ Jesus, being one with the Father, must of necessity possess this attribute. Without being immutable, Christ could not lay claim to deity nor sonship with the Father. Being the God of both heaven and earth from all eternity, change in Him is impossible. He could not change if He wanted to, and He cannot want to if He could. If there were the slightest possibility of change, it would render Christ unworthy of being God.

From Christ, no attribute ever passes away, be it communicable or incommunicable. He effects change, but He Himself is not affected by the changes. Whatever changes take place in any realm, whether in the celestial or the terrestrial, Christ is unchanged.

Eternity, with all its years, stands present before His all-seeing eyes. And what do we know about eternity? Nothing! We are not here long enough to learn much about time. How, then, can we know anything about eternity or the eternity of being?

In time, there is no abiding present, and in eternity, there is neither past nor future. In eternity, everything is an ever-abiding now. Eternity has no gray hairs. The Word lies down in the sepulcher of the ages, but time writes no wrinkles in the brow of eternity. Time plows no furrows in the face of the eternal now. From all eternity, Christ stands eternally glorious in His own divine perfections without being bound by the ties of yesterday, today, and tomorrow.

He is not a creature of time, nor can He be bound by the laws of time, nor affected by circumstances that arise in the annals of time, whether it be decades, centuries, or millenniums. As finite creatures, we live in a world of change and changes.

Time changes. The atmosphere changes, and seasons change. The moon changes, and customs change. Traditions change, and methods change. Neighborhoods, communities, and cities change. Living conditions change. Systems, cultures, and civilizations change. Our friends, children, and our parents change. Our bodies and our faces change. Husbands, wives, brothers, and sisters change.

Men change their minds, their associates, their lifestyles, and their habits. Men change their vocations, their dress, their outlook on life, and their pursuits in life. Men change their appointments, their views, their positions, their stations in life, their ways, and their religious beliefs. Men change their church affiliations, their homes, their names, and their priorities. Men are subject to shock and frustration, lose heart, and wreck their future. Men become discouraged and lose interest. Men are right today and wrong tomorrow. Men can be good today and bad tomorrow. Men can be friends today and foes tomorrow. Men can be kind today and cruel tomorrow. Men can be angels today and demons tomorrow. Men can be sympathetic today and cold in heart tomorrow. Men are up today and down tomorrow. Men can be happy today and sad tomorrow.

God gave man life, but He did not exempt him or rid him of the freedom of choice and changes. Man changes from a noble man to a nobody to a somebody. Man is one way today and another way tomorrow.

But this is not the way with Christ; He remains the same. He is not subject to change and changes. His life does not wax and wane. He does not gain new powers nor lose those which He has hid from all eternity. He does not mature nor develop. He does not grow stronger or weaker. He does not grow wiser with the passing of time. He is the all-wise God from all eternity; He does not have to learn; He is the omniscient God. He cannot change for better or for worse, for He is absolutely perfect.

The fundamental difference between Christ and man is that man is mutable, and his human nature renders him subject to change and changes. Strain and shock and circumstances can and do alter the character of man, but nothing and no circumstance can affect nor alter the pure, unblemished character of Christ.

The character of Christ today is exactly as it is eternally. We change from the birth to the final hour of death. The bloom of youth gives place to the strength and vigor of manhood. The strength and vigor of manhood eventually gives way under the burden of old age. The eyes grow dim by reason of strain and years. The hair is painted white like the frost of winter. The back becomes bent with life's heavy load. Steps that were once nimble and quick are slowed down to a toddling pace and sometimes to a sudden halt by a stroke of paralysis. The voice that was once strong and clear becomes a whisper. The ears become hard of hearing, and familiar voices become strange and unrecognizable. Dimpled cheeks are plowed into furrows by the unerring hand of time. The grinders cease to thoroughly masticate food because they are few or not at all. The mind that was once sharp and keen becomes dull, and memory plays us false and sometimes completely slips away from us, even in our youth.

Sickness slips upon us without notice, and we linger helpless on a bed until the inevitable day of death. Our best laid plans are often defeated by unfavorable and unrelenting foes. Trouble seems to come out of nowhere for no reason at all. The clock of time ticks away our years in a hurry, even if they be fourscore and ten, plus. We come upon the stage of action, say our speech, the curtains of life are drawn, and the drama of life is over. But this is not the case with Christ. He will ever remain the same, and His years have no end.

In Psalm 110:3, it is written concerning Him, "Thou hast the dew of thy youth." The scientists tell us that this world is growing old. The Bible tells us that, one day, the sun will burn itself out, the moon will one day drip away in blood, and the stars will fall from their sockets like figs falling from a fit tree when shaken by the wind.

The Bible tells us that, one day, the heavens will depart as a scroll when it is rolled together. The Bible declares that the earth will burn with a fervent heat and melt like wax before the all-engulfing flame. The Bible declares that, one day, the mountains in the distant yonder, which rest their rock-ribbed brows on the bosom of the floating clouds, will fail and come to naught. The Bible says that the age-old rocks which are embedded in the mountains will lose their solidarity and be reduced to dust.

The Bible says that the little hills will vanish from sight and the sky will crack like glass. The seas will boil like a pot on fire. The Bible says that, one day, time will be no more. But of Christ, the Bible says that He remaineth forever and His years fail not. He is Alpha and Omega; He is the beginning and the end. He is the first and the last; He was God manifested in the flesh, seen of angels, justified in the Spirit and preached unto the Gentiles. He is Mary's baby, the light of the world, the tender plant of renown, the first-born among many brothers, the light unto the Gentiles, the true light shining in a dark world, the King who cannot be dethroned, and the crowned Prince who wears a spotless robe. He is the bright morning star that never wanes. He is the sun of righteousness that never sets and the all-conquering King who has never lost one battle.

Matthew traces His genealogy from Abraham to His foster father Joseph. This covers a period of 42 generations. But He, whose genealogy Matthew traces back to father Abraham in time, is the timeless one that times the time and the times. He said Himself, "Before Abraham was, I am."

The old hymnologist wrote concerning Him: "Before the hills in order stood or earth received her frame. From everlasting thou art God, to endless years the same."

In the prophecy of Isaiah, He says, "I am the Lord. That is my name and my glory will I not give to another, nor my praises to graven images." What Christ was in eternity, He did not cease to be in time. A thousand ages in His sight is like an evening gone. Eternity will all its years stand present in His view. To Him, nothing old appears. Great God! There's nothing new. What He was in eternity, He was in time. And when time shall cease to be, He will ever remain the same. The psalmist asks, "O Lord! Who is like unto Thee? The heavens are thine, the earth is thine also. Thou ruleth the raging of the seas and stills the dashing waves thereof." Great is the Lord. There is none like unto Him. The Lord reigneth. He is clothed with majesty. The Lord is clothed with strength. His throne is established of old. He is from everlasting to everlasting. The Lord reigneth; let the earth rejoice. Let the multitude of the isles be glad.

In the Book of Revelation, He is the old which is, which was, and is to come. He is not a human prodigy. He was God manifested in the flesh. In Him dwelt the fullness of the Godhead. His birth was an occasion too glorious for men to announce and an occasion too great for angels to keep secret.

Being heaven-planned, heaven-timed, and heaven-sent, Christ could not hide His identity. That solitary, starlit night when He was born in Bethlehem, angels stood in midair, singing, "Glory to God in the highest; On earth, peace and good will to men."

Even though there were no midwives around when Christ was born to help Mary while in hard labor, He was born the fairest among ten thousand, altogether.

Dr. Lee says, "His every nerve was a divine handwriting. His every bone was of a divine sculpture, His every heartbeat was a divine pulsation. His every breath was a holy whisper. Divine omnipotence moved in His arms, divine wisdom was cradled in His brain, divine love throbbed in His heart, divine compassion glistened in His eyes, divine grace was in His soul, divine mercy was in His hands to help, divine pity was in His heart to forgive, and divine power was in His will to heal. To give eternal life to all who will believe was His divine purpose and a divine halo of glory was upon His brow."

Thus, in John, John sees Christ being more than the son of Mary and Joseph. He sees Him as being more than a carpenter's son. He sees Him as being more than a worker of miracles and wonders. He sees Him as being more than a local itinerant preacher and teacher. He sees Him being more than a common man. He sees Him being more than a lover of children. He sees Him being more than a helper of the helpless and the infirmed.

John sees Him as being the eternal logos, existing eternally with the Father. He sees Him as being the eternal one. John sees Christ as the self-existent one. John sees Him as the everlasting one, and he sees Him as the coming one. Note he says, "That which was from the beginning." The verb "was" means that which was already in existence, that which had no beginning. He was and is before there was a beginning or ever the beginning was begun. His "was" and His "is" equal His eternal "isness." The prophet Micah says He has ever been of old.

Again, the old hymnologist wrote:
"O God our help in ages past
Our hope for years to come
Our shelter from the stormy blast
And our eternal home.

Before the hills in order stood
Or earth received her frame
From everlasting thou art God
To endless years the same.

A thousand ages in thy sight
Is like an evening gone
Short is the watch that ends the night
Before a setting sun."

Solomon says of Christ in his proverb, "The Lord possessed me in the beginning of his way; Before His works of old, I was set up from everlasting." You see, what Christ was before He came to earth, He did not cease to be when He came to earth. He did not lose His place in the Godhead. In time, He did not become any less God than He was in eternity. He is the same today, yesterday, and forever.

Though He was the Son of Man on earth, He remained the great God of eternity. One has well said that, when Jesus came to earth to redeem the world, He was as much man as though He was not God and as much God as though He was not man.

You remember that He said, "Before Abraham was, I Am." In Solomon's song, He says, "I am the rose of Sharon, and the lily of the valleys." In the Gospel of John, He said, "I am the good shepherd." At Jacob's well, He said that He was the well of living water. On the backside of the desert, He said, "I am the living bread."

He is the same in redemption, the same in salvation, the same in grace, the same in justification, and the same in sanctification. He is the same in love, the same in truth, the same in kindness, and the same in goodness. He is the same in benevolence, in tenderness, in gentleness, the same in His providence, the same in patience, and the same in longsuffering. He is the same in preservation, the same in bestowing blessings, the same in His graciousness, the same in His consideration, and the same in His eternal purposes. He is the same in His godliness, in His godlikeness, in His timelessness, and the same in His everlastingness.

He is the same in His absoluteness, in His divine perfections, in His fidelity, in His dependability, and in His trustworthiness. He is the same in His faithfulness, in His effectiveness, in His impartiality, in His divine assurance, and in His chastisement. He is the same in His comfort, the same in His counsel, the same in His consoling, the same in His justice, the same in His forgiveness, and the same in His tolerance. He is the same in His understanding, in His demands, in His commands, in His reprimanding, in His unwavering, in His unwariness, and in His watchfulness. He is the same in His waiting, in His rebukes, in His reparation, in His denouncement, and in His bounty. He is true to His word. He is faithful to all of His promises, and He is marvelous in His merits. He is the great I AM of eternity, God's only Son, and He is the first begotten from the dead.

The same man gave sight to the blind, unstopped deaf ears, and fed the hungry. This same man healed the sick, raised the dead, and cleansed vile lepers. This same man calmed raging seas, walked on the water, expelled demons, and blessed little children. This same man ate with publicans and sinners, prayed for His enemies, and dried blinding tears. This same man walked the dusty roads, climbed the rocky steeps on mountainsides, and rode a beast of burden. This same man caused the crippled to walk, unloosed stammering tongues, turned water to wine, and preached the Gospel of repentance. This same man carried a cross to Calvary, died an ignominious death on that old rugged cross, was buried in a borrowed grave, and rose triumphant from the grave. This same man sent men forth to preach the Gospel, ascended to heaven on a cloud, is now seated at the right hand of God the Father, and gives eternal salvation to all believers.

This same man untied my hands, saved my soul, and set me free. This same man saved my life, keeps me saved, and keeps me safe. This same man is my watchman day and night, feeds me when I am hungry, and catches me when I fall. This same man fights my battles for me, is my shield and buckler, my hope and stay, and my light and my salvation. This same man is the joy of my salvation, the strength of my life, and the Lord of my life. This same man is my shepherd, my protection, and my shelter from the stormy blasts of life. This same man keeps my soul from danger. This same man has all power in Heaven and in earth in His hands.

There is nothing high and noble and sublime, that He is not. To the artist, He is altogether lovely. To the architect, He is the designer of both heaven and earth. To the carpenter, He is the master builder. To the baker, He is the Bread of life. To the hungry, He is the living bread. To the thirsty, He is the well of living water. To the banker, He is the hidden treasure. To the investor, He is the pearl of great price. To the philanthropist, He is God's unspeakable gift. To the wise, He is wisdom personified. To the educator, He is the teacher come from God. To the student, He is the inexhaustible subject. To the farmer, He is the seed of the woman, the seed of Abraham, the stem of Jesse, the seed of David, and the sower going forth to sow. To the florist, He is the rose of Sharon, the lily of the valley. To the astronomer, He is the sun of righteousness, the star of David, the bright morning star, and the brightness of the Father's glory.

To the doctor, He is the great physician. To the judge, He is the righteous judge. To the lawyer, He is the author of jurisprudence. To the jurors, He is the faithful witness. To the geologist, He is Daniel's rolling stone, the smitten rock at Mt. Horeb, the rock of defense, the rock of ages, the shadow of a great rock in a weary land, the stone which the builders rejected, and the chief cornerstone.

To the prodigal, He is the way to the Father's house. To the traveler, He is the true and living way. To the sinner, He is the seeking Savior. To the Christian, He is the author and finisher of our Faith. He is the joy of our salvation.

There are no needs that He cannot supply, no hurts that He cannot heal, and no broken hearts that He cannot mend. There are no sorrows that He cannot soothe, no tears that He cannot dry, and no problems that He cannot solve. There is no load that He cannot lift, no burdens that He cannot bear, no depth that He cannot reach, and no heights above Him. There is no soul that He does not love, no stains of sin that His blood cannot remove, and no repentant sinners that He will not forgive.

His character is unreproachable, and His love unlimited. His righteousness is untarnished, and His grace is sufficient. His promises are sure, and His mercies are new every morning. His faithfulness reacheth unto the clouds, and His goodness is to all mankind because He is changeless, and in Him, there is eternal stability.

MY NAME IS REVEREND THORN

2 Corinthians 12:1-7

Hello, my name is Reverend Thorn. Nobody knows my pedigree or ancestry. Nobody knows who my mother is or who my father is. Nobody knows from whence I've come. All that is really known about me is that I am a paradoxical, unconventional minister. I have never been to seminary. I don't have any degrees. I don't have a local parish. I don't even get any kind of remuneration. I am just an itinerant minister who goes from place to place. I am a paradoxical minister because I am a messenger of Satan but I do my ministry by the permission of God.

I'm not like Jesus and Dr. Martin Luther King. I am not nonviolent. In fact, I am very violent. To be honest, I am brutal, I fight, I hurt, and I cause excruciating pain. But though I am brutal, and though I cause excruciating pain, I am a beneficial, preventive minister. People really don't care for me. Although people don't like me because of my brutality, I prevent greater cataclysmic disasters. It is because of my brutal ministry that I don't get invitations to conduct revivals, seminars, and conferences like other ministers. But though they don't like me nor invite me, I am a needful and necessary minister. I am a needful and necessary minister because, even though I am brutal, I am a minister who keeps God from enacting and inflicting His judgment. I am a minister who keeps God from honoring His word.

Now, the interesting thing about my ministry is that the only way you can hear me preach is that you have to have an unusual endowment, or you have to receive an extraordinary blessing. Another interesting thing is that, when I preach, I don't have to have but one sermon. If you don't mind, I would like for you to hear me at my classic best.

Let me begin my story by setting the stage. There was a man who temporarily made a stop in the ancient city of Macedonia. While in that city, he wrote his fourth letter to the Christian church that was in the city of Corinth. In that letter, he made it clear to the people that he was troubled. He was troubled because of an experience that had happened to him somewhere between A.D. 42 and A.D. 44.

What happened was that somewhere between A.D. 42 and A.D. 44, this troubled, tossed writer had an experience which was based upon revelation. This man's experience was ineffable or indescribable. This experience was mysterious ecstasy. It was mysterious because the word mystery in its truest form does not lose its mysteriousness even after it has been revealed. And we know it was ecstasy because ecstasy means standing outside of one's self, and it occurs when a man is grasped by the ultimate mystery.

I'll tell you what, in order for you to get a close-up view, let me step aside and call the man who heard me at my level best. My name is Paul the apostle. I have been called from glory by Reverend Thorn to tell you of my experience with him. In order for me to tell you the story, I must begin at the beginning.

I know that Reverend Thorn has given you the prelude to my story, but what even he does not know is that, in order for me to talk about my story, I have to talk about it like it was somebody else, even though I know that that somebody was me. I can tell you about my ecstatic, ineffable experience, but I cannot give you any minute details. The most that I can tell you is where I was. I was in the third heaven. And when you understand that there are three distinct heavens, and they are the abode of the clouds, the abode of the solar system, and the abode of God, then you come to understand exactly where I was. I was in the third heaven, which means that I was in the abode of God. It is at this point that I introduce you to:

I. My Prideful Problem

When you read verses 2-4 of 2 Corinthians 12, you will see that my problem was that I had had a third heaven experience. My third heaven experience represents an unusual endowment. To show you that it was an unusual endowment, I had a third heaven experience and escaped with my life. That's unusual. For the record is that Enoch walked with God, and God took him. After wrestling at Peniel, Jacob astonishingly cried, "I have seen God face to face, and my life is preserved." Moses reports that God said to him, "You cannot see My face; for no man shall see me, and live." When Gideon realized who his visitor had been, he cried in terror, "Alas, O Lord God! for because I have seen an angel of the Lord face to face." And God's reply to him was, "Peace be unto thee; fear not; thou shalt not die." When Manoah discovered that the messenger who had brought him the news of the coming birth of a son was an angel of the Lord, his terrified reaction was, "We shall surely die, because we have seen God."

Jewish tradition has it that there are four rabbis who claimed to have had visions of God. Ben Azai saw the glory of God, and he died. Ben Soma saw the glory, and he went mad. Acher beheld the glory, and he became a heretic. Akiba was the only who was said to have ascended in peace.

So, you can see that I had an unusual endowment. My unusual endowment was not only one that I had had a third heaven experience, but I also escaped with my life. Because I'm just like other men, I have perverted nature, and because of this, unusual endowments are not only blessings, but they are problems. The problem that I have is twofold; one is that there is temptation to become lifted up in pride. When men have unusual endowments, there is the perennial temptation to become arrogant. Unusual endowments will make you self-sufficient. They will incite you to resist depending upon God. They will cause you to shun divine assistance. The ultimate problem with pride and arrogance is that they wind up driving a wedge between you and God.

Unusual endowments have a way of reducing God and increasing "I." The middle letter of sin and pride is "I." The bigger the "I" in pride, the bigger the sin. Do you really know what a cross is? A cross is really a crossed out "I." That's why following Christ involves denying "I." God hates pride and arrogance, and it is vented in His Word, for it says, "Pride goes before destruction, and a haughty spirit before a fall."

That's what happened in the Adam and Eve situation. When Satan convinced Eve that eating from the forbidden tree would make them as gods, he was appealing to the pride of life. And when they did eat, it drove a wedge between them and God. The Bible plainly says that God hates pride and arrogance. The reason God hates pride is because ultimately pride will cause you not to reverence God. Pride has a way of making you disregard your duty toward God. Pride has a way of making you despise and look down on others in disrespect. When we fail to reverence God and then look down with disrespect and contempt on our fellow brother, then we really do have a problem. Proverbs 16:18 says "Pride goeth before destruction, and an haughty spirit before a fall." Then Proverbs 29:23 says, "A man's pride shall bring him low." Then Jeremiah 50:32 says that "The most proud shall stumble and fall, and none shall raise him up." So based upon these scriptures, the real problem of pride is that pride is inextricably tied to disaster. When you talk about falling and destruction, that's disaster.

My problem was that, if my unusual endowments incite me to become arrogant, I have a problem because pride becomes an open invitation to disaster and destruction. When we read verse 6, we come to understand that I had a second problem. The latter part of verse 6 tells my second problem. It says, "Lest any man should think of me above that which he seeth me to be, or that he heareth of me." The other half of the problem is that, when we have unusual endowments, people will become mesmerized and preoccupied with the external and the spectacular.

If we are not careful, men will wind up deifying us because of our unusual endowments. That's why so many young people are in trouble in the 20th century. They become impressed with the person who has the unusual endowments. It is my understanding that a 20th-century man named Malcolm X deified a man called Elijah Mohammed, and he was almost destroyed when he discovered that the man that he had deified was a man of the flesh with weaknesses and frailty. It is a real problem when men start deifying other men because, when men deify men, we soon worship whom we deify. When we start worshiping deified men, we are on a collision course with God. God gets jealous because He wants worship and devotion for Himself alone. So, when God's jealousy is stirred, His wrath becomes kindled, and His kindled wrath issues into divine judgment. When we have to deal with God's wrath issuing into divine judgment, we have a problem. Therefore, my second problem was prohibiting men from deifying me because of my unusual endowment.

II. My Preventive Pain

It is at this juncture that I was introduced to Reverend Thorn. I met him as my preventive pain. Verse 7 says, "And lest I should be exalted above measure through the abundance of the revelations, there was given to me a thorn in the flesh, the messenger of Satan to buffet me, lest I should be exalted above measure." Before I look at the idea of my preventive pain, let me point out something; and that is, notice that my ecstatic experience was not ongoing. I'm convinced that it was not ongoing because man does not have the capacity to endure any extended period of transcendent glory. Man does not have the capacity to endure and withstand ongoing glory. Like God did for Isaiah, He permits us to see His train. As God told Moses, I will let you see my backparts, but you cannot see my face. I have come to find out that man can't even handle God's train, and God's backparts. I'm convinced that one of the reasons Jesus did not allow his three disciples to remain on the mountain is because man does not have the capacity to handle ongoing transcendent glory. In order for us to handle ongoing transcendent glory, we must have new celestial bodies.

Another thing to point out is that, as soon as I came out of ecstasy, I was introduced to Reverend Thorn. It's interesting that I had one ecstatic experience, but I have been dealing with painful Reverend Thorn for 14 years. I hate to tell you, but that's how the life of a Christian really is. You always have more pain than ecstasy. Pain lasts longer than ecstasy. Ecstasy is episodic. You have rapturous events every now and then, but pain is perpetual and ongoing. What this says is that man is better equipped to handle perpetual pain than he is ongoing transcendent, rapturous, ecstatic glory.

Then, I've come to realize that, when God introduces you to Reverend Thorn, He always has a beneficial purpose. This brings us to the question, why is it necessary that we meet Reverend Thorn? Before I answer, let me just say that scholars have tried to identify just what Reverend Thorn looks like. Some say that he looked like physical weariness, some say physical pain, some say opposition, some say slander, some say severe headaches, some say epilepsy, some say carnal temptations, and some say that he looks like an eye disease called chronic ophthalmia which is an inflammation of the eyes.

And after all of these years, men still don't know his true identity because he has kind of a chameleon personality. He just keeps changing with the environment. Sometimes he looks like sickness, and sometimes he looks like grief. Sometimes he looks like financial difficulty, and sometimes he looks like unsolvable problems. Sometimes he looks like trials and tribulations, and sometimes he looks like marital disruption. Sometimes he looks like disobedient children, and sometimes he looks like a church that refuses to follow godly leadership. Sometimes he looks like carnal-minded people who oppose the idea of being pastored. Sometimes he looks like somebody that you have helped who has turned on you. Sometimes he looks like an overly ambitious young preacher. That's why I was conspicuously silent as to what he looks like. But, though I was silent about what Reverend Thorn looks like, one thing I was not silent about, and that was that he deals out excruciating pain. The question is, for what purpose did I meet Reverend Thorn? I met Reverend Thorn so that he could "buffet" me lest I got "exalted above measure." I think I need to tell you that the pain Reverend Thorn inflicted on me was accompanied by rationality. But, when we compare my pain with Brother Job's pain, we shall discover that pain is not always accompanied by rationality. When we look at Job's pain, we see that part of Job's pain was the irrationality of his pain. So what this says is that there will be times when we know why we have pain, and then there will be times when we have to suffer in the dark. But, the one thing we must be assured of is whether pain is God-sent or God-allowed, God always causes pain to work for His glory and our ultimate good. That ultimate good is to conform us to the very image of Jesus Christ. You see, we are God's glorification project, and what God will do is use the pain that is dealt out by Reverend Thorn to conform us to the image of Christ.

So it is at this point that we see the needfulness of Reverend Thorn. In order to see the needfulness of Reverend Thorn, we must understand the word "buffet," and we must understand the word "thorn." The word "thorn" means "a stake," and the word "buffet" means "to brutally treat." So, what this says is that Reverend Thorn, who is also known as Reverend Stake, treats me brutally.

Let me put it to you this way; it is said that the higher a ship's superstructure reaches into the sky, the heavier it has to be on the bottom. So, in order to keep the ship from lifting up out of the water, toppling, and eventually sinking, the ship builder has to place heavy weights in the hull of the ship.

The issue is that I had an unusual endowment. I was susceptible to becoming top heavy. The mechanism to offset me from becoming top heavy and eventually toppling over was Reverend Thorn, who would brutally treat me. And it appears that every time I became susceptible to pride, that's when I would hear Reverend Thorn preach his only sermon, which consists of one line, and that is "You'd better get back down."

Now, what this says is that buffeting, brutal Reverend Thorn is a minister of God. When we get great blessings, and it seems that we are tempted to get caught up in pride, conceit, vanity, self-dependence, and self-sufficiency, and when it looks like we are about to get top heavy, we too will be introduced to Reverend Thorn. And, we too will hear his one message, and that is, "You had better get back down." I might as well tell you that the higher you ascend, the more unusual your endowments, the greater your blessings, the more you will hear from Reverend Thorn. Be careful about desiring great blessings because, with great blessings, comes great pain.

Let me conclude my story by telling you that you can cope with Reverence Thorn.

III. My Perfect Provision

In verse 8, I tell you that I went to the Lord on three different occasions, asking the Lord to remove the thorn. "I besought the Lord." And the word "besought" is the same word as "paraclete." The word "paraclete" means to call along side, which means then that I called the Lord along side of me to remove the thorn. On three different occasions, God said, "No." In this ordeal, I found out that God will tell you no, but I also found out that God's noes are not cold and frigid. God's noes are bathed in benevolence, saturated in sensitivity, loaded with love, and grounded in grace.

What we must come to grips with is the fact that God is sovereign, omniscient, and omnipresent. This says that God always knows what is best for us. But look how the Lord follows up His noes. He said, "My grace is sufficient." The word "grace" here means enabling power. The phrase "is sufficient" means that "we'll be content." What this means is that God has enough enabling power to provide you with adequate contentment in the midst of your pain.

It is at this point that I have made a remarkable discovery, that my strength is made perfect in weakness. When we link this statement with the hurting that is inflicted by Reverend Thorn, we come to understand that the affliction caused by Reverend Thorn hurts, but it does not render us ineffective. We must understand that trouble which is caused by Reverend Thorn, at its best, is troublesome, but it does not render us ineffective. And I know that's so because effectiveness is not based upon human ability. Effectiveness is based upon the omnipotent ability of God. Too many people are sitting idle, doing nothing because they have become preoccupied and enthralled with their lack of ability. But what we must understand is that God has never asked for ability. He asks only for availability. God asked Isaiah, "Whom shall I send, and who will go for us?" That's asking for availability.

Too many of us are just like Moses. We spend all of our time talking about our lack of ability, and God is saying, "I don't need ability. I have all of the ability I need. I have all power at my disposal; but what I want is for you to merge your availability with my ability." But now, somewhere along the line, I accepted God's answer, and I know that I accepted God's answer because I had a mood change. That's when I said, "Most gladly, therefore, will I rather glory in my infirmities, that the power of Christ may rest upon me." My mood swing helped me to say, "I take pleasure in infirmities, in necessities, in persecutions, in distresses for Christ's sake."

Look at what happens. I go from pleading for the removal of Reverend Thorn in my life to boasting and delighting about my weaknesses. I can boast and delight about by weakness. I can boast and delight about my weakness because when I am weak, then am I strong. Some rationalists want to know, "How can you be strong when in fact you are weak?" The fact is, we can become strong when we are weak by admitting our own insufficiency and then by leaning upon the sufficiency and the enabling power of God's grace.

And this is where God wants us. He wants us where we have no other choice but to lean on Him. I have found out that God will orchestrate situations and circumstances whereby there is nobody else to lean on but Him. I've come to find out the real meaning of the hymn:

"What a fellowship, what a joy divine; leaning on the everlasting arms!

What a blessedness, what a peace is mine; leaning on the everlasting arms!

Oh, how sweet to walk in the pilgrim way; leaning on the everlasting arms!

Oh how bright the path grows from day to day; leaning on the everlasting arms!"

When we rely upon God's enabling grace, we can go from pain to praise. Notice that I start out in pain, but I end up in praise. No, I am not praising because of the pain inflicted by Reverend Thorn, but I am praising God because of His grace in the midst of my pain. I'm not praising because I'm hurting, but I'm praising because of the help that I got from my hurt.

I've come to find out that, when we realize that God's grace is help and enablement for our inadequacies, when we realize that His grace is sufficient, then we don't have to wait until all is well to praise Him. We can praise Him when all is not well.

We can praise Him when we are down.

We can praise Him when we are sick.

We can praise Him when we are grieving.

We can praise Him when our enemies are around.

We can praise Him when our home is in turmoil.

We can praise Him when our marriage is shaky.

We can praise Him when our children won't do right.

We can praise Him when our money is funny and our change is strange.

We can praise Him when our bills are due and we don't have a dime.

We can praise Him in the midst of a storm.

We can praise Him when we are in the valley.

We can praise Him when it seems all hope is gone.

Reverend Thorn and Paul, I thank you for your contributions, but I think I can take it from here. "When waves of afflictions sweep over the soul and sunlight is hidden from view, if ever you are tempted to fret or complain, just think of His goodness to you."

THE OLD GOSPEL FOR NEW TIMES

Romans 1:16; 1 Timothy 1:15

T. Harwood Pattison, in his book entitled *The Making of the Sermon* says, "Gospel preaching is the promulgation, or proclamation of divine truth, with view to persuasion." For the Gospel, as it relates to eternal salvation, there is no substitute. God has set the seal of His everlastingness upon it and declared it to be the only way of salvation and entrance into His kingdom. If there is no adherence to the Gospel, there is no eternal salvation, no justification, no sanctification, no adoption into the royal family, and no final glorification at the second coming of Christ. It demands repentance toward God on the part of the sinner and his exercise of simple faith in Jesus as the Savior who alone has eternal salvation to give.

In Matthew 24:14, it is called "the gospel of the kingdom." In Acts 15:7, it is called "the word of the gospel." In Acts 20:24, Paul calls it "the gospel of God's grace." In Romans 1:9, Paul calls it, "the gospel of [God's] son." In Romans 1:16, Paul calls it "the power of God unto salvation." In Romans 10:8, Paul calls it the gospel "of faith." In Romans 10:15 he calls it "the gospel of peace." In Romans 15:19, he calls it "the gospel of Christ." In Romans 15:16, he calls it "the gospel of God." In 2 Corinthians, Paul calls it "the light of the glorious gospel." In Galatians 2:7, he calls it "the gospel of circumcision." In Colossians 1:5 he calls it the gospel "of truth." In Colossians 1:23, he calls it "the hope of the gospel." In 2 Corinthians 5:18, Paul calls it the gospel "of reconciliation." In Hebrews 8:13, it is called the gospel of the "new covenant." And, in Revelation 14:6, it is called, "the everlasting gospel."

The angel that appeared to the shepherds that solitary, starlit night on the plains of Judea when Jesus was born in Bethlehem called it Good News and glad news. The Gospel is both Good News and glad news from the high heavens. The Gospel is the newest news and the most newsworthy that has ever reached the ears and hearts of men of earth since news had its inception. Although almost twenty centuries have passed since the Gospel's dispensation began, the Gospel of Christ is still new and news.

It is fresher than the morning dew and newsier than the newest news. It is news from heaven to the inhabitants of an old earth. It is Good News and glad news from a far country. The Gospel is the truth of God revealed in Christ who is the express image of the Father. It is Heaven's message of salvation for lost men of earth through the blood of Christ. The Gospel is heaven's welcome home to the outcast. The Gospel is a message of hope to the despairing. The Gospel is heaven's panacea for a sin-sick, devil-ridden world. The Gospel is heaven's invitation to hungry and starving souls from the heavenly Father to the banquet table. The Gospel is manna from on high. The Gospel is water for thirsty and famishing souls. The Gospel is Heaven's light for a world of darkness. The Gospel is the living Word from the living God to dying men that they might live. The Gospel is God's warning of judgment to rebellious, hardhearted, and unrepenting sinners.

While the Gospel tells of God's undying love in the giving of His only begotten Son to die, it does not fail to point out the horrors of hell, where the ungodly must spend eternity. While the Gospel tells of the glories of heaven, it is quick to tell about the lake of fire which burns continuously in hell. The Gospel is that sweet, old story that will never grow old. It is the sweetest and the greatest story ever told. It is the most interesting and most valuable story ever told. It is the truest story ever told. It is the only story written anywhere which tells of God's undying love for lost men. It is told more often than any other story. It is told by more people than any other story. It is told in more places than any other story.

Like a scarlet thread, this story runs through the Bible from Genesis through Revelation. It will never grow old while the light of hope is kindled on the bosom of the future and undaunted faith is fueled at the altar of her God. The Gospel story is the story of eternal salvation through and by the blood of Christ. It was designed in heaven by the Godhead to convince and convert sinners to the point that they will come to Christ by faith in Him for salvation. It was designed to reclaim backsliders, to edify the saints, to spiritually enlighten and enliven Christians, and to strengthen those who are weak. It was designed to give courage to the strong to persevere, to declare God's righteousness and His love for mankind. It was designed to feed hungry, starving souls, to be a light unto the Gentiles, and a lamp unto the feet of all believers. This Gospel emerged to warn sinners of the coming judgment, the horrors of hell, to prepare true believers for the entrance and the enjoyment of the glories of heaven.

The Gospel saves, condemns, it draws, and it drives. It praises, blames, hurts, and it heals. It wounds, and it makes whole. It excites, frightens, persuades, it offends. It consoles, and it disturbs. Like a two-edged sword, it cuts right and left. It cuts going and coming. It cuts even between the joint, marrow, and bones. It is appealing, and it is offensive.

The Gospel reaches into our innermost being when it is preached with power and shows us our true and sinful selves. It uncovers our secret sins and shows them to us that we might see ourselves as we really are. The Gospel brings some to repentance and faith, and others who are hard-hearted go heedlessly to an early death and to an untimely grave. Salvation through Christ, by the power of the Gospel, includes repentance and faith and the cleansing of the human conscience. It includes the cleansing of the heart by the washing of the Word and the forgiveness of sins. It is God declaring the guilty innocent and delivering souls from death. It is the restoration of our relationship with God by the blood of the cross and our adoption into God's royal family. It declares justification by faith and daily sanctification by the Word. It provides fellowship with believers, membership in the New Testament Church, and guidance by the Holy Spirit. The Gospel continues to provide guardian angels round about us and free access to the Father.

Although the Gospel is often ignored; it stands unmoved and untarnished. No man ever wins an argument against the Gospel, no matter how learned he may be. Whatever men say against it does not change it. It says what it means and means what it says. Its message remains the same from one generation to the next generation until generations are no more. The Gospel will outlast time and remain fresh and powerful in the business of salvation as long as a sinner remains to be saved, a backslider to be reclaimed, and one saved soul remains to be nourished by the Word.

The Gospel story is the story that the prophets of old foretold. It is the impregnable rock upon which they anchored their hopes. Salvation by the blood of Christ is the story that no other story tells. It must be the text of every God-called preacher, even in the most crucial hours and dangerous situations with nothing doubting.

The Gospel makes preachers out of infidels, believers out of agnostics, deacons out of gamblers, and choir members out of blues singers. It makes honest trustees out of thieves and calls strumpets from the streets. The Gospel of salvation, through the precious, pure, and redeeming blood of Christ, made Christian martyrs of the early Church give their lives unflinchingly. Salvation, through the blood of Christ, was the eternal purpose of Calvary and the crucible of the cross upon which Jesus died.

The Gospel is the explanation of that which took place in heaven in the Determinate Council of the Godhead, when the plan of world redemption and man's eternal salvation were discussed by the Godhead eons before this terrestrial ball upon which life was ever ushered from the womb of chaos. Salvation, through the blood of Christ, is the sum total of regeneration, justification, sanctification, adoption, preservation, and final glorification. Salvation, through the blood of Christ, is the mystery that had been hid in

God from all eternity. It is the revelation of that mystery that the angels desired to look into but were forbidden. If the angels had been permitted, they would not have understood it anyway because of their limitations. Angels cannot understand the eternal working of the omniscient, omnipotent, and infallible mind of the divine.

World redemption and eternal salvation by the power of the Gospel is the Gospel story capsuled in the blood of the cross. With God, the Gospel story is no idle tale. With God, the Gospel story is serious business and infinitely more than human rhetoric. It is more than a Sunday speech, an oration, and more than a well-written poem. It is more than the preacher's well-written manuscript and more profound than the human eloquence of delivery.

With God, the Gospel is no play thing. He does not take it lightly. God emptied Himself for men's salvation in giving His only begotten Son to die on Calvary for Him to take it lightly. He has set the seal of His eternal guarantee upon its accomplishments when preached in its purity.

The central figure of the Gospel is Christ. Its most glorious attraction is the cross. Its most magnified spot is a hill called Calvary. The burden of the Gospel hangs upon the horrible, shameful, ignominious death that Jesus died and reaches its crescendo in His glorious resurrection, His ascension, and His intercession.

The power of the Gospel is in its regenerating, soul-reviving, and life-transforming influence on the souls and lives of believers. The proof of the Gospel is the Gospel itself. The benefit of the Gospel comes when man believes and accepts it by faith. The scope of the Gospel is the whole world. The purpose of the Gospel is to save sinners. The boundary of the Gospel is to the end of time. The marvel of the Gospel is, although it is centuries old, it has never lost its charm nor power to save.

The glory of the Gospel is Christ and His cross. The aim of the Gospel is to call men and women and boys and girls from darkness into the marvelous light of Christ. Salvation, by the power of the Gospel, makes us new creatures in Christ Jesus, and it reconciles us to God. Salvation, by the power of the Gospel, changes our state and standing with God, gives us peace with God, changes our lifestyle, and changes our minds. It alters our thinking, our desires, our attitudes, and our disposition. The power of the Gospel changes our outlook on life, redirects our path, rectifies our lives, and pricks our consciences. It makes us careful about our conduct, shames us when we sin, and disturbs the soul when we err.

Salvation, by the blood of Christ, finds us utterly lost in sin and restores us to God's loving favor. It finds us broken and makes us whole. It finds us defiled and cleanses our hearts. It finds us strangers and takes us into God's loving sheepfold. It finds us dead in sin and makes us alive in Jesus Christ. It finds us aliens and adopts us into God's royal family. It finds us condemned and reverses the decision. It finds us sinners and declares us saints. It finds us guilty and grants us pardon. It finds us hell bound and re-routes us to heaven.

The Gospel story, being the story of world redemption, must be seen and heard in the light of the bloody scene at Calvary. If we miss Calvary, we have missed it. At Calvary, unholy men trampled their unholy feet in the blood of the sinless Lamb of God, feeling no guilt or remorse of conscience. Those who mocked Jesus with their would-be comical genuflection on the way to Calvary took it as a holiday.

To the Roman soldiers, it was considered a duty. To the disciples of Jesus, it was a seeming defeat and a sad disappointment. To Mary, the mother of Jesus, it was heartbreaking, but to Jesus, it was the fulfillment of a promise— the promise which He made to the Godhead in eternity. Jesus left heaven with Calvary on His mind and a cross in His view. Although His crucifixion was a dreadful sin, it was no surprise or shock to Him. He left heaven with world redemption on His mind, and there was no other way but by the cross.

To many persons today, the cross is only an ornament on their person as an impressive emblem in a fruitless effort to symbolize saintliness. To the skeptics, the cross symbolizes superstition and fearfulness on the part of the weak-minded folks, but the cross of Jesus is more than an ornament. It is more than a gold stickpin and more than a bracelet. It is more than a watch fob. It is more than a picture on the wall. It is more than a painting in stained glass windows. It is more than a sculptor can chisel in stone. His cross was not wreathed with flowers.

The cross of Jesus was an old, rugged cross made of wood. It was a heavy cross. His cross meant death, and death in any language is not a pretty subject. Although it meant death for Jesus, it meant life, and it still means life to all who will believe. His death was a tragic death, but His tragic death meant triumph over death. When Jesus died on the cross, the cross of tragedy became the cross of hope. The cross of shame became the cross of honor. The cross of penalty became the cross of pardon. The cross of darkness became the cross of light. The cross of condemnation became the cross of redemption. The cross of seeming defeat became the cross of victory.

When the angels looked upon the bloody scene, as Jesus hung upon the cross, they were awed beyond expression. Lest we forget, much was involved in the death of Christ on that cross; there were underlying love and divinity on the Cross. There were forgiveness and reconciliation on the Cross. There were divine compassion and spiritual light on the Cross. There were justification and soul-reviving power on the Cross. There were adoption provision, peace, and eternal security on the Cross.

Now, let me tell you what is contemporaneous about the Cross. There is still divine love and divine mercy in the Cross. There is forgiveness and life-giving power in the Cross. There is still spiritual light in the Cross and justification in the Cross. There is still amazing, saving grace and eternal security in the Cross. The Cross is the way to the Father's heart, to the Father's treasures, and the way to the Father's house.

What a glorious Gospel we have to preach! Preaching has always been God's method when calling sinful men back to Himself, and it will be His method until the last man in the most distant regions of the earth has had a chance to hear it.

Where there is no preaching, there is no repentance. Where there is no preaching, there is no return of prodigals, no calling of prostitutes from their waywardness, no Christian homes, no church, and ultimately no preachers.

But what would we do without the illustrious chronicle of proclaimers in the Bible? Let's check the Old Testament record:

Noah, Abraham, Melchizedek, Moses, Aaron, Joshua, Caleb, Samuel, Elijah, Elisha, Jonah.

The chronology continues because Gideon preached, Amos, Hezekiah, Micah, Obadiah, Nathan, Josiah, Ezra, Isaiah, Jeremiah, Ezekiel, and Daniel preached.

Closing the Old Testament, Hosea preached, Joel, Nahum, Haggai, Jehu, Nehemiah, Zephaniah, Zechariah, Solomon, and Malachi preached. Asa, Eli, Mordecai, Jonathan, Job and Jesse. All of these Old Testament saints, sages, and prophets had a message from God to individuals and nations, calling them to repentance.

The unfolding of the New Testament drama is characterized by prolific preachers who went forth as flames of fire, proclaiming the Gospel of eternal salvation. Peter, James John, Mark, and Nathaniel preached. Likewise, Matthew, Luke, Thomas, Philip, Silas, Rufus, Archipus, Barnabas, and Paul preached. Paul's sons in the ministry continued the legacy of proclamation.

Timothy and Titus preached. Justus, Didymus, Jason, Ananias, Jude, Cornelius, and Simeon preached. And finally, Philemon, Tychicus, Eubulus, Trophemus, Apollos, and Artemus preached.

When Jesus heard that John the Baptist was in prison, He came forth preaching, and what a preacher! Herod thought that, if he could silence

John, preaching days would be over. He thought that, if he put John in jail, there would be no disturbing voice from the wilderness. He thought that, if he put John in jail, there would be no more questions about his guilt, and if he locked up the old town crier, there would be no one coming to the wilderness to hear him. Herod thought if he put John in jail, there would be no gathering or congregation on the banks of the Jordan, and if he quieted John, there would be no one to trouble his conscience and no one else to meddle in his licentious affairs.

But what Herod did not know was that there was a man called Jesus Christ coming after John who was mightier than he, whose shoelaces John felt unworthy to untie; a man who would preach a Gospel of repentance and eternal salvation with a power that John never possessed. This man, Jesus, would preach a Gospel never before heard of. This man, Jesus, would preach a Gospel of salvation and eternal damnation. His Gospel would draw and drive and bless and damn.

But, the world has not changed much since the days of Herod nor since the days of the prophets. The world is saying today, "Make the preacher hush his mouth, and there will be no one to either challenge or condemn us for our godless pursuits. If we get rid of the preacher, there will be no gospel of repentance ringing in our ears. If we can outlaw prayer in school, let incorrigibleness, lawlessness, crime, and dropouts, dope and dope pushers, dope addicts, and winebibbers and let homosexuals take over, we won't need a Gospel or preachers to preach."

Take the Bible and the family altar out of every home, and children will grow up without any regard or respect for parents because they will have no religious training and no reverence for God. If we let little children stay in bed on Sunday morning or roam the streets and alleys rather than be in Sunday school and church, they will end up in prison as hardened criminals or fill untimely graves.

If we get rid of the preacher, there will be no disturbing voice to prick our conscience. If we silence the preacher's mouth, there will be nothing and nobody to remind us of the horrors of hell. If we get rid of the preacher, jerk the deacon up off of his knees in prayer, kill the musician at the organ and break up the choir with petty jealousy, there will be no prophetic voices to call us to repentance. If we break in and interrupt the public worship any way we can, bring about confusion in the membership, burn the church, leave the membership out of doors with no place to call their church home, and split the membership and make them lifetime enemies of each other, men and women will refuse to hear the Gospel. Remember! It happened during the days of the early Church.

Listen to the record of the early Church: put John the Baptist in jail, crucify Jesus on a cross, saw James asunder, crucify Peter with head down and heels up, banish John to the Isle called Patmos.

Dissension raised its ugly head and said to stone Stephen to death, scatter the church at Jerusalem, beat Paul unmercifully, lock Paul and Silas in the dungeon, and forbid Paul to preach before the city council.

The strange voices get louder as they say to make Demas a deserter, plan a midnight assassination of Paul, bring about a dispute between Paul and John Mark, make Peter and Paul fall out over the doctrine, leave Paul in jail without a coat or a blanket, and cut off Paul's head at the chopping block, and the Gospel will no longer exist.

But lest we forget, we must remind our opposition about the power of the Gospel on the kerygmatic side of the ledger. We must remind them about what happened to the prophets who prophesied of a coming Messiah and the Gospel age and tell them what happened to Elijah. We must make them mindful of Jeremiah's dungeon and Daniel's lion's den. We must tell them what happened to the three Hebrew boys, but more importantly, we must be sure to tell them how Jesus was crucified.

Paul writes, "How can they hear without a preacher?" Eternal life hangs upon the Gospel. The Gospel is the balancing power of the world. Christ and His cross must forever remain the subject of the Gospel. His death, burial, resurrection, and ascension must remain its central theme.

We must preach Christ.

We must preach about Calvary.

We must preach about the cross.

We must preach world redemption by blood.

We must preach salvation by grace.

We must preach justification by faith.

We must preach the Gospel of atonement.

We must preach sanctification by the washing of water by the Word.

We must preach one Lord, one faith, and one baptism.

Though we might want to outlaw and outmode it, the Gospel will remain relevant and potent until the day Jesus comes. It is old yet ever new. It will never grow old as along as there remains one sinner to bow at the altar, begging for salvation. It will never grow old as long as there remains one backslider to return home. It will never grow old as long as there remains one spiritually blind man coming to Jesus, seeking the touch of His finger for spiritual sight. It will never grow old as long as there remains one vile leper coming to Jesus for cleansing. It will never grow old as long as hearse wheels roll and mourners go about the streets. It will never grow old while the light of hope is kindled on the bosom of the future and while faith is fueled and the altar of her God feeds her eternal fires.

The sun may go down in sackcloth of hair.
The moon may drip itself away in blood.
The stars may fall from their sockets.
The earth may burn with a fervent heat.
The seas may boil like a pot on fire,
But the Gospel will remain potent until the coming of Christ.

This is the glorious Gospel we preach. This is the old, old story we must tell. This Gospel saves sinners. This Gospel rebuilds broken lives. This Gospel mends broken hearts. This Gospel builds Christian character. This Gospel shapes and molds young lives. This Gospel builds church houses. This Gospel builds Christian schools. This Gospel keeps families from falling apart.

This is the Gospel that Peter preached at Pentecost. This is the Gospel he preached in the home of Cornelius. This is the Gospel that James preached in Jerusalem. This is the Gospel that Stephen preached, though he was stoned to death. This is the Gospel that Philip preached in Samaria and which he preached to the eunuch. This is the Gospel that the early Church preached. This is the Gospel that Paul preached in Athens, in Rome, in Berea, in Thessalonica, in Corinth, in Ephesus, in Troas, in Galatia, in Crete, in Decapolis, in Phonecia, on the river banks, on Mars Hill, in his tent shop, before Festus, before Felix, before Agrippa, before Caesar, and before King Herod. And this is the Gospel we must preach and preach unashamed.

I become ashamed of myself but not of the Gospel. I get sick of me sometimes but not of the Gospel. I get disgusted with me at times but not with the Gospel. I get tired of my blunders but not of the Gospel. I become ashamed of my conduct at times but not of the Gospel. I get ashamed of my human weakness at times but not of the Gospel. I become ashamed of my attitude at times but never ashamed of the Gospel. I become ashamed of my wandering thoughts but never ashamed of the Gospel. I become ashamed of my slothfulness at times but not ashamed of the Gospel. In the light of God's holiness, I get ashamed when I think about my unworthiness to preach, but never am I ashamed of the Gospel. I become ashamed of my powerlessness in preaching but not of the Gospel.

This is a glorious Gospel. This Gospel challenges the deepest thinkers and brings kings and nobles to their knees. This Gospel makes governors tremble, rocks empires, and braves the rage of lions. This Gospel quenches the violence of fire, calls sinners to repentance, and makes high heads bow and haughty spirits humble. This Gospel makes strong men out of weaklings, bad men good, mean men kind, and proud men graceful. This Gospel makes evil men pure in heart, gives hope to the despairing, courage to the strong, strength to the weak, and grace to the humble. It lifts the fallen, feeds hungry, starving souls, and is water for the thirsty soul. It is bread from heaven, the manna from on high, which sets prisoners free and unclouds the mind. This Gospel illuminates the understanding, consecrates the will, straightens the thinking, and governs the temper. This Gospel controls the actions and bridles the tongue, purifies the soul, and brightens the countenance. It brings peace to the inward man, dignifies the personality, beautifies life, and makes life worthwhile. This Gospel sanctifies the whole man, makes one able to stand in the hours of crisis, brings joy in the midst of sorrow, and relieves old hatred. This Gospel banishes all fears, relieves mental pressure, opens spiritually blinded eyes, removes all doubts, and makes one hold fast to that which is good. It is this Gospel which makes one aspire for that which is high, makes one look on the bright side of life, and makes one tenderhearted. This Gospel of Jesus Christ gives one respect for others, guides the footsteps, holds the reins of the mind, and makes believers anxious to do God's will. The Gospel of Christ Jesus lifts one to higher heights, makes one strive for the best, and prepares believers for heaven.

Don't be ashamed of the Gospel!

JESUS CLASHES WITH THE DEVIL IN CHURCH
Mark 1:21-28

There are some people who are under the grave misnomer and erroneous conviction that the church of Jesus Christ ought to be friction free. They believe that, since they encounter friction at home, in the street, on the job, and in school, the one place that there ought to be an obvious absence of friction is in the church. They are convinced that the church is no place for friction, conflict, and confrontation. But, anybody who believes that there won't be friction, clash, and conflict in the church is sleeping with an illusion. It's an impossibility for the church to be friction free. For, if you were to find a friction-free church, the moment that you walk in, that would cancel that because you are walking friction. You are a walking tug of war. The church will not be friction free until Jesus comes.

Another reason that there will be inevitable conflict in the church is because two conflicting, divergent, and diametrically opposite forces show up at one time in the same place. Anytime the church gathers, just know that the godly and the satanic have gathered. And when the forces of the godly and the satanic meet in the same location, there is bound to be conflict and confrontation.

Take note of the fact that, whenever there is conflict, the conflict ought to always be between opposing forces. There is never to be confrontation between the allies. The church, however, is being victimized by the "Little Black Sambo" syndrome. The task of the church is to oppose the enemy wherever the enemy shows up. But, it is obvious that we are not following the Bible posture because there is evidence that we engage all of our time, and we exhaust all of our energy and time, strategizing against our allies. It's a sad factor that the true enemy remains unscathed and undefeated because we spend the bulk of our time warring and killing off our teammates.

As a believer, when you fight me, that's not warfare because I'm on the same team. That's self-flagellation; that's self-mutilation; that's self-destruction; that's ecclesiastical cannibalism; that's consuming and devouring one another. It's tragic that we, as the church, are not battling the true enemy, but we are brawling with one another.

And Paul says in Galatians 5:15, "But if ye bite and devour one another, take heed that ye be not consumed one of another."

Perhaps we don't know who our battle is with. So, maybe I will tell you what Paul said. Paul said, "We wrestle not against flesh and blood, but against principalities, against powers, against the rulers of the darkness of this world, against spiritual wickedness in high places." If, then, you are conflicting with fellow believers, your fight is against the wrong target, and you are just wasting time. Your warfare is with the prince of the power of the air, who is Satan, his emissaries, the world, and the flesh. We need to recognize who our true enemy is and, thus, cease brawling and combating with each other.

There are even some people who seem to feel that conflicts and clashes in the church are some new phenomena. I will to suggest that it has been that way a long time. Job 1:6 proves it as it says, "Now there was a day when the sons of God came to present themselves before the Lord, and Satan came also among them." And, our text is also undeniable proof that conflict in the church is nothing new.

In our text, we see Jesus clashing with the enemy. Now, the place where Jesus clashes with the enemy is in the synagogue.

The origin of the synagogue is shrouded in mystery. Traditionally, it is believed that the synagogue originated around 581 B.C. when the Jews were in Babylonian captivity, at which time they were deprived of the Temple worship. As a result, they assembled together for worship in this strange land in a place they called "synagogue."

1. By the first century, the synagogue was a well-established institution. Ten heads of Jewish households could establish a synagogue.

2. The synagogue did not compete, rival, or create a problem with the Temple. Because, even though the Temple provided a facility for teaching, the main emphasis of the Temple was offerings and sacrifices, while the emphasis of the synagogue was reading and explaining Scripture, prayer, and worship.

3. The synagogue was structured in such a way that in the very center of the synagogue was an elevated platform upon which stood a reading desk. Worshippers sat upon wooden seats which surrounded this elevated platform.

4. I think it is also interesting to note the fact that the synagogue always faced Jerusalem. It was built in such a way that the speaker, while addressing the audience, and the audience when leaving, was always looking toward the Holy City. Thus, the Galilean synagogues faced south; the synagogues east of the Jordan faced west; those synagogues south of Jerusalem faced north; and those synagogues west of Jerusalem faced east.

What this meant then was that, every time Jesus preached in the synagogue, He was always facing the place where He was going to be crucified. So then it was impossible for Him not to think about His ultimate destination, which was Calvary and the Cross.

The order of worship was thanksgiving in connection with the Shema, prayer, and the reading of a passage from the Pentateuch and then from the prophets.

5. Then, there was the scripture exposition. The person who was to give the sermon or scripture exposition would stand upon the elevated platform and read from a standing position behind the reading desk. After reading the scripture, he would then sit and explain the scripture that he had just read. And finally, the priest would give the benediction.

So now, having some insight as to the goings on in the synagogue, we come to the text.

Mark records what seems to have been a memorable Sabbath. The first incident that occurred on this memorable Sabbath was in the synagogue in Capernaum, which was the home of Simon Peter, and which Jesus used as a base of operation for His Galilean ministry. As the custom of Jesus was, on the Sabbath, He went to this particular synagogue and, undoubtedly, was invited by one of the synagogue leaders to preach. And, the first thing that we see from this synagogue experience is:

I. His Masterful Proclamation

Although Mark does not afford us with the contents of Jesus' proclamation, we do know that it was masterful. We know it because of a) the authority of His speaking, b) the astonishment of the people, and c) the affright of the demonic.

The Bible said that Jesus spoke with authority. Some people have inherited authority. Some people have delegated authority. Other people have achieved authority. But, Jesus has inherent authority. What this means is that Jesus does not have authority because of an office because He has no office. His authority is in and of Himself. He has authority because of who He is. He is deity personified. This means that He has underived authority. His authority is in His pure and holy personhood. Because of the fact that He is God in the flesh, and because He possesses the twin attributes of omniscience and omnisapience, it is not necessary for Him to quote anybody.

There is a silent contrast here. And that silent contrast is between Jesus and the teachers of the Law. In that contrast, you will see that Jesus did not have to do like the scribes. He did not borrow from fallible sources. He did not buttress or bolster His arguments by quoting from some scholars. He did not rely upon the expositions of His predecessors. He cites no authorities. He did not live in the rhetorical prison house of quotation marks. In fact, Jesus did not even say "thus saith the Lord," but He spoke knowing that He needed no authority beyond Himself. He spoke in a voice of finality. He drew from His own being. He spoke with authority of one who knew. He spoke from His own mind. He acknowledged no master and no superior. His manner was special and unique. His matter had eternal ramifications, infinite height, cosmological depth. He was the very source of His authority. In fact, He was authority personified. That's why He says, "Ye have heard that it was said, but I say unto you." That's authoritative.

And if Jesus' preaching is masterful preaching, then perhaps we need to re-evaluate and re-assess what we perceive as masterful preaching. You see, Jesus' authority was spiritual and omnipotent. Ours seems to be less spiritual and human. It seems as though, like the ancient scribes, we quote everybody but Jesus. I think it's fine to be acquainted with the arguments and postures of the great theologians but never to the exclusion of Jesus. You see, the arguments of the great theologians may be jewels, but they might be indigestible jewels because Jesus may not be its very center. I don't care what kind of nugget it might be; if Jesus is not the center and citadel of it, the soul classifies it as a reject. We wonder why people hear us preach and then leave hungry and thirsty. It could be because it contains no Jesus substance. If our preaching is to be food and substance for hungry souls and drink for thirsty spirits, then it must be Jesus centered.

If we preach Jesus, we have authority and substance for the soul. If we preach Jesus, the Lord will give us delegated *dunamis*, or power.

But then, look at the astonishment of the people. The Bible said that "they were astonished." It is of interest to know that the literal definition of a miracle is "that which produces astonishment." And the word "astonished" means "to be stung by a lick." And the preaching of Jesus was a miracle because it was an event which was stinging, astonishing, and caused shaking. And then to say that they were astonished is to say that Jesus' proclamation was so miraculous until, like being stung, it made a prolonged impact upon those who heard Him.

And again, I affirm the fact that, if Jesus' preaching is masterful, then we need to re-assess and re-evaluate what we perceive to be masterful preaching. You see, our preaching promotes ecclesiastical "rousology" and emotional stirring. Our preaching causes people to jump high when they shout rather than to walk straight when they come down. When we finish preaching, it is like chewing gum—a lot of motion but no real progress. It's like clouds without water—all promise and no substance. But nobody seems astonished. There is not the prolonged impact. In fact, we can preach now, and in a little while, what we preached about will be forgotten. It could be that no one is astonished at our preaching because we who preach are not sufficiently astonished. If we were more astonished, maybe we could do more astonishing. And, I have found that astonishment begins not in the active voice but in the passive voice. When I think of the breathtaking miracle that God loves me, with all of my frailty, sins, weaknesses, and shortcomings, so much so that He sent His Son to die in my stead, I ought to be astonished. And then, when I think about His supernatural rationale for calling me to preach, I am astonished again. So, what happens is that my passive voice, which has been nurtured by revelation, influences my active voice. And, when that happens, the revelation in my passive voice incites an ecstasy in my active voice, so when I preach, I'm in a state of ecstatic astonishment. Which means that I have a severe case of "I can't help myself." So, when I preach from a state of ecstatic astonishment, somebody ought to be astonished because astonishment is catchy and infectious. So, somebody ought to get stung by a lick. There ought to be prolonged impact.

And finally, we know it was masterful because of the affright of the demon. The Bible said that the demon "cried out." Take note of the fact that Jesus did not go into the Synagogue looking for the man. But, He went into the synagogue to masterfully proclaim the Word. And, when He proclaimed the Word with power, the demon became uncomfortable, affrighted, and cried out. The demon was tortured with truth.

For a third time, I say that if Jesus' proclamation is masterful, then we need to re-evaluate and re-assess our perception of masterful preaching because it seems that, when we preach, the demonic are not affrighted. The demagogic are not aggravated. You see, Jesus' preaching affrights, aggravates, and disturbs evil. Jesus' preaching dislodges the devil. Jesus' preaching agitated demons. When Jesus is preached, devils can't be still. When Jesus is preached, peaceful demons who possess souls and rule lives start crying out.

So then, I will to suggest that, if our preaching is to be masterful, it must be crammed with Christ, adorned in His authority, able to disturb devils, and proclaimed with power. And, when you finish, somebody ought to be so stung that they ought to want to conform to the image of Christ.

In the synagogue in Capernaum, not only are we exposed to Jesus' masterful proclamation, but we see Him exhibiting:

II. His Mighty Power

The record is that the synagogue service was suddenly interrupted by a man "possessed by an evil spirit." It is obvious that the presence of Jesus and His authoritative powerful proclamation evoked a strong outburst from this man that was under the control of this "evil spirit." I think we should understand that the physical utterance was that of the man's vocal organs, but the man himself was not the speaker. The speaker was the spirit who possessed the man. Now, there are a couple of things that stick out here.

a. The Recognition of the Demon

This unclean spirit recognized that he was in the presence of unsullied or undefiled holiness. He recognized Jesus' ministry in the world. Take note of the fact that there was only one unclean spirit in the man. But the unclean spirit uses the plural as he says to Jesus, "You have come into the world to destroy us." The demon realizes the fact that the kingdom of evil will imminently be destroyed. This demon clearly recognizes the judgment ministry of Jesus.

But, not only does he recognize Jesus' ministry, but he:

b. He Recognizes the Person of Jesus

Notice, he calls Jesus, "Jesus of Nazareth." He recognizes Jesus' true character, for he called Him the "Holy One of God." There are a couple of things that need to be pointed out here. First of all, it should be noted that it is useless to have a mere intellectual knowledge of religion. The devil cries out, "I know thee who thou art." He had knowledge, but it was not unto salvation. Mere belief of the facts and doctrines of the church will not save you. Such a belief is no better than the belief of devils. They believe that He is the Holy One of God, the Son of God, and the Son of the most high God. James says that devils believe and tremble, but there is no salvation.

What we need is a head knowledge that issues into heart belief, love, and trust. A knowledge that results in total, mystical, chimaerism, reciprocal indwelling, and that's hypostatis union. It's about total engrafting. I'm in Him, and He's in me. I'm in the vine, and the vine is in me. And, this issues forth into speaking in possessive pronouns. The Lord is my Shepherd. The Lord is my light and my salvation. The Lord is my rock and my fortress. The Lord is my shield. The Lord is my refuge and strength, a very present help in trouble. The Lord is my God. The Lord is my exceeding great reward. The Lord is my inheritance. The Lord is my blesser. The Lord is my provider. The Lord is my caretaker. The Lord is my deliverer. The Lord is my high tower. The Lord is my lamp. The Lord is my Savior.

But then, secondly, by way of contrast, isn't it strange that the unclean spirit knew Jesus' name and His true nature? And, when you contrast the evil spirits' recognition of Jesus, knowing that they are beyond mercy, with man who is the object of mercy, compare the demons' recognition of Jesus with the recognition of man, who was made by Jesus and whom Jesus came to save. And, it is a shock that man does not know the true identity of his Maker and Savior. But as the little children sing, "Everybody Ought to

Know Who Jesus Is." And for man, knowing who Jesus is is rather important. It is important because it is the difference between life and death, heav-
en and hell, salvation or damnation, lost and found, bound or free, rescued
or perishing. And, because of the fact that knowing Jesus has eternal ramifications, everybody ought to know who Jesus is.

But, look at Jesus' response to the unclean spirit's recognition. Jesus
rebuked him. Jesus was aware of two things. One was that He did not want
evil testifying on His behalf because, if evil testifies on His behalf, it gives the
appearance that He is in league with evil. That would discredit the credibil-
ity and veracity of the ministry of Jesus. And, Jesus did not want to give the
impression that He was an ally of evil. He did not want people thinking that
He had engaged Himself in some unholy alliance. He wanted it to be very
clear that true holiness and evil are enemies. Jesus wants it to be known that
there can be no affinity between holiness and evil. Jesus wants it to be clear
that there is a deep antagonism between God and the devil. Therefore, Jesus
could not receive a testimony from a diabolical demagogic source.

And, I think one of the problems with the modern church is that it is not
clear that we are enemies with evil. One of the problems with the Vietnam
War was the fact that you could not distinguish the difference between the
enemies and the allies. So, as citizens of the kingdom of God, we ought not
to be looking like we are of the kingdom of evil.

But then, Jesus was also aware of the fact that holiness and evil are mutually repellent. There is no way that they can co-exist. That's why Lucifer was
thrown out of heaven. You wonder why you are a walking tug of war. You
wonder why we must have changed bodies when we go to heaven; holiness
and evil are mutually repellent. The fact is that holiness and evil cannot co-
exist. And, let me just say that, if you want to cancel evil in your life, get
more holiness. I'm not talking about pharisaic, hypocritical self-righteousness, but what I'm talking about is getting more Holy Ghost. And, the more
Holy Ghost you get, the more you start conforming to the image of Jesus
Christ. The more Holy Ghost you get, the more you will surrender to the
Lordship of Christ. The more Holy Ghost you get, the more you die to sin
and self. The more Holy Ghost you get, the more you look like Jesus. The
more Holy Ghost you get, the less evil you will have on the inside.

I think that we should understand that confrontation and conflict and
clashing was inevitable at this point because of the fact that the devil was in
two places where he did not naturally belong. He was in the man, and he
was in the church. He does not naturally belong in man because man was
not made for devil possession and demagogic usurpation, nor was the church

established for demonic intrusion and infiltration. Man was made a God look-a-like, designed to glorify God, and the church was established to evangelize the sinner, edify the saint, elevate society, and exalt the Savior.

So, knowing that true holiness and evil are mutually repellent, and knowing that the devil is in two places where he does not belong, Jesus goes from rebuking the evil spirit to exorcising or making him come out of the man. That's miraculous, mighty power. And, take note of the fact that Jesus exhibited this kind of power before He stood on resurrection ground and said "all power," which tells me that He has the power to handle whatever infirmity I may have. I want to tell you today that Jesus has power.

He has power to save, power to heal, power to raise up a bowed down head, power to give joy in sorrow, peace in confusion, and hope in despair.

But now, I want you to pay close attention to something. In verse 26, it says "and when the unclean spirit had torn him, and cried with a loud voice, he came out of him." The fact is, when an evil tenant is compelled to leave, he frequently shows his spite by damaging the premises. Satan cannot win, but he can tear. The demon showed his rage at being disembodied by throwing the man into a convulsive spasm. Now, the evil spirit did not do permanent damage, but he did tear him on the way out. When Satan loses his hold on you, he does all that he can to harm you. What the devil cannot keep as his own, he seeks to destroy. Satan tempts, plagues, and buffets more fiercely when he is losing his tyranny.

The record is that, when the children of Israel were about to be emancipated from Egypt, Pharaoh increased their burdens. The point is that, as long as you are unconscious, unconcerned, and careless about sin, Satan will leave you in peace. But, the moment you seek salvation or become concerned about true holiness, Satan will try to tear you. But the good news is that, when Satan starts tearing on you, you know that he is on his way out. He never starts trying to do major harm until he knows that he is on his way out. Let me ask you something. Have you had a feeling that the devil was tearing at you? Have you felt him seeking to do you harm? Do you feel like you have been fiercely tempted? Does it seem like you are being buffeted and tossed about? Does it seem that you are having to deal with one severe plague after another?

Does it seem that your burdens are heavier? He's on his way out.

Does it look like he is raining down havoc in your life? He's on his way out.

Does it look like he's sifting you real hard? He's on his way out.

Does it look like he's causing more destruction than ever? He's on his way out.

Does it look like he's stirring up more trouble than ever before? He's on his way out?

Does it look like he's causing more unrest? He's on his way out.

When the devil loses his grip, he tears you on his way out.

Finally, because of His masterful proclamation and His mighty power, Jesus was the recipient of:

III. His Marvelous Popularity

The Bible says immediately His fame spread abroad. That word "fame" means "report," which means that the report or word about Jesus went out in all directions. They spread the news over the whole region of Galilee, which means that His notoriety was connected to their report. They reported His doctrine and His deeds; His Word and His works; His proclamation and His power; His message and His might; His authority and His actions. They reported that He was an authoritative teacher. That's who He is. They reported that He is an almighty deliver. That's what he does.

I don't know about you, but I try to add to Jesus' notoriety by reporting what I know. Well, I'm reporting that I know who He is. He is the one who is adorned in authority, girded in grace, mantled in majesty, robed in righteousness, vested in virtue. He's the one who is glorious in His grace, judicious in His justice, kind in His kingliness, limitless in His Lordship, matchless in His might, precious in His peace, pre-eminent in His power, resplendent in His renown, righteous in His reign, sufficient in His salvation, sure in His sustentation. He is the beginning of the beginning, He is the uncaused causative cause, He is the one who spoke and it was done, commanded and it stood fast.

That's who He is, but I also know some things that He can do:

He can heal your body.

He can lead you to life.

He can make you whole.

He can restore your soul.

He can unburden your heart.

He can regulate your mind.

He can liberate your spirit.

He can set you free.

He can forgive your sins.

He can renew your strength.

He can deliver you from distress.

He can make the devil leave you alone.

He can right your wrong.

He can rescue the perishing.
He can care for the dying.
He can make all things new.
He can give you new life.
He can give you a new heart.
He can give you a new spirit.
He can give you a new mind.

That's why Paul said, "If any man be in Christ, he is a new creature; old things are passed away, and, behold all things are become new." And, I am a witness. Because, one Wednesday evening, He made me new. I heard the voice of Jesus say, "Come unto me and rest."

THE SERMON ON THE MOUNT
"Blessed are the merciful: for they shall obtain mercy."
Matthew 5:7

In my study of the Beatitudes, I have discovered that some of the Beatitudes look up right away into heaven; others of them look down into all the relations of earth and time. In other words, some of the Beatitudes are intensively theological and others are intensively moral and social. Thus, in the Beatitudes, we have a complete representation of the religion which Jesus came to establish and expand, a religion combining the theological with the moral, the doctrinal with the practical, and God with His creatures (neighbors).

In the Beatitudes, Jesus makes it clear that, in the Christian religion, earth and heaven go together. In the conception of the blessed life, goodness and reward always go together.

"Blessed are the merciful: for they shall obtain mercy," (Matthew 5:7). Mercy means compassion, kindness, forbearance, benevolence, pity, clemency, humanness, softheartedness, tolerance, charity, grace, leniency, sparing, exorable, indulgent, kind, gentle, moderate, touched, humanitarian, forgiving, mildness, pardon, fellow feeling, long-suffering, placable, light sentence, tender, plea for pity, understanding, condole, witty, to spare, to be slow to anger, to allow time for repentance, not to be hard upon, to melt, to thaw, to be graceful, to give a second chance, to have sympathy, to be understanding, to be lenient with an offender, to scorn taking revenge, tenderhearted, beneficent, and inwardly affected with the infirmities and miseries of others, feeling them as their own, and endeavoring to help relieve them.

Mercy does not only mean to sympathize with a person, and it does not mean simply to feel sorrow for someone in trouble. Mercy means the ability to get right inside of the other person's skin until we can see with his eyes, think things with his mind, and feel things with his feelings.

Mercy is much more than an emotional wave of pity. Plenty of folk can feel sorrow for you, but mercy means to be sorry enough to do something about it. Mercy means to have a deliberate identification with other people until we can see things as they see them and until we can feel things as they feel them. Mercy means to experience things together with other people, to be experiencing what they are experiencing.

Mercy means to have inward empathy which produces an outward act to help relieve the sorrow and suffering of others. In the story of the Good

Samaritan, the preachers felt something, but they did nothing, but the Samaritan looked and responded. Many times, we see injustices and do nothing, but mercy responds and comes to the rescue.

The word "mercy," as used by Jesus in the text, is also seen in its historic and positive meaning. Mercy is a word based on the Hebrew word "che/se/dh" used frequently in the Old Testament to express the unique quality of the everlasting mercy of Jehovah God. That's why, when things happen, we cry, "Lord, have mercy. Have mercy!" The word carries the meaning of identification in the suffering of others, of going through something with another, or entering into another's problem with understanding and acceptance. This is what God did for us in Christ, identifying with humanity and suffering on behalf of our sin. Jesus was 100 percent God, yet 100 percent man. He was God and man, or the God-man.

That's why Jesus can identify with us because He was at all points tempted like we are, yet He did not sin. Jesus knows, Jesus sees, and Jesus understands! "Blessed are the merciful: for they shall obtain mercy."

Mercy is the exercise of less severity than one deserves, the granting of kindness or favor beyond what one may rightly deserve. Mercy is forgiveness and pardon exercised toward the ill-deserving. Pardon remits the outward penalty which the offender deserves. Forgiveness dismisses the act from the heart of the one offended. Mercy seeks the highest possible good for the offender. Mercy is kind and compassionate treatment in a case where severity is merited and expected. Mercy is the granting of kindness or favor beyond what one may rightly claim. Mercy has to do with grace, and grace is kindness and favor or blessing shown to the undeserving.

Mercy is grace in action. Mercy is love reaching out to help those who are helpless and who need salvation. Mercy identifies with the miserable in their misery. Mercy is a holy disposition in contract with that foolish sentimentality which flints the requirements of justice. Mercy is more than feeling; it is an operative principle. Mercy not only strikes the heart, but it moves the hand to render help to those in need. Mercy is a copious source of acts of beneficence from which issue streams of blessings. Mercy does not exhaust itself in profitless words but is accompanied by helpful deeds. Mercy is a proceed from an inward passion.

Blessed are the merciful. Blessed are those who show mercy, and blessed are those who extend sympathy. Those who express love, those who are willing to forgive, and those who show mercy will be shown mercy. Those who forgive will be forgiven.

We are to forgive one another as God has forgiven us. Jesus taught that, to be forgiven, we must be forgiving. The condition of my being forgiven is that I forgive. In the model prayer that we call the Lord's Prayer, Jesus said, "forgive us our debts, as we forgive our debtors." The merciful are they who forgive as they are forgiven.

The merciful are not only merciful in action, but they are to be merciful in disposition. Followers of Jesus must be men and women of mercy who affirm we have found mercy and mercy has found us. Having thus found mercy, we become the channel to convey mercy. "Blessed are the merciful: for they shall obtain mercy." Because they have already obtained mercy; therefore, they are merciful. We must not only experience the mercy of God, we must express the mercy of God. Mercy is the reward of mercy.

The merciful are those who possess that spontaneous overflow of the heart that is captivated by and in love with the mercy of God. Mercy does not originate in the human heart and then proceed toward God. Mercy originates with God and is then showered upon men. Mercy is unforced and unmerited. It comes from God to the undeserving. Mercy comes to us from God not because of what we are but because of who God is. Mercy is not a reward for what we are but is an expression of God's loving and gracious concern for those who are the object of His affection. "Blessed are the merciful." The merciful person is the one who is full of the fountain of mercy. This merciful man is a man that is full of God, full of love, full of compassion. God is the source of mercy.

Psalm 86:15 says that God is "plenteous in mercy."

Psalm 90:14 affirms, "O satisfy us early with thy mercy."

Psalm 107:1 - "O give thanks unto the Lord, for he is good: for his mercy endureth forever."

Psalm 119:64 - "The earth, O Lord, is full of thy mercy."

Micah 7:18 says, "He delighteth in mercy."

Ephesians 2:4 says, "God ... is rich in mercy."

Psalm 89:1 - "Sing of the mercies of the Lord..."

Psalm 103:8 - "The Lord is merciful and gracious, slow to anger..."

Psalm 103:17 - "The mercy of the Lord is from everlasting to everlasting..."

Psalm 109:21 - "Thy mercy is good."

Psalm 119:156 - "Great are thy tender mercies..."

Psalm 130:7 - "With the Lord there is mercy..."

Jeremiah 3:12 - "'I am merciful,' saith the Lord."

Daniel 9:9 - "To the Lord our God belong mercies and forgivenesses."

2 Corinthians 1:3 - Paul declares that God is the "Father of mercies, and the God of all comfort."

Mercy is God's loving grace in action. Mercy is God's response to the misery and need of the one whom He loves. In the mercy of God, God has not dealt with us "after our sins; nor rewarded us according to our iniquities," (Psalm 103:10), but rather God deals with us not in terms of what we are but graciously, in spite of what we are. Love and grace are combined in what the Bible calls the mercy of God. If God marked our sins, we could not stand in His sight because, in our sinfulness, we have no acceptance before Him. God in grace, however, sets aside what we deserve in order to give us what we could never deserve. This is what theologians call existentialism. God extends Himself beyond our circumstance. He extends Himself to use where we are and takes us to where we should be. The old folk just said, "He looked beyond my faults and saw my needs," or "If it had not been for the Lord on my side, where would I be?"

When man sinned in the Garden, divine justice decreed that man must die, but mercy said, "Give him another chance." Because of God's mercy, a search warrant was sent out and inquired who will go on man's bond?

Noah's building program was not enough.

Abraham's faith could not see far enough.

Job's patience was not patient enough.

Jacob's all night wrestling match did not settle enough.

Enoch's walking with God was not straight enough.

Moses' rod did not reach far enough.

David's music was not sweet enough.

Elijah's altar on Mt. Carmel was not sacrificial enough.

Solomon's wisdom was not wise enough.

Isaiah's prophesies were not prophetic enough.

Jeremiah could not cry loud enough.

Ezekiel's wheel did not spin fast enough.

Daniel's prophetic utterance was not enough.

Amos' plumb line was not straight enough.

Malachi's tithe could not buy enough.

Matthew's taxes could not pay enough.

John the Baptist could not cry loud enough.

Mercy in the person of Jesus came. Jesus became the personification of the mercy of God. For three years, He healed the sick and raised the dead. He resorted lunatics to reason, calmed the storm with the words, "Peace, be still," and cast out devils. He opened blinded eyes and broke up funeral processions. He caused helpless cripples to throw their crutches away and unstopped deaf ears. Jesus loosed stammering tongues of the dumb and astonished the doctors and lawyers. He found remedies for the hungry by telling them "I am the bread of life," and He offered life for physical death, "I am the resurrection and the life." For the cripple, He gave new limbs and cleansed the lepers. He mended broken hearts and raised bowed heads. Jesus made graveyards picnic grounds and made angry seas peaceful and calm. He saved sinners, reclaimed backsliders, and sent the devil running.

The church is marching on. Friday, He went to Calvary and died. He would not come down from the cross. He decided to die on the cross. That is why the hymn writer writes, "At the cross, at the cross, where I first saw the light, and the burden of my heart rolled away. It was there by faith, I received my sight, and now I am happy all the day."

THE SERMON ON THE MOUNT
"Blessed are they that mourn: for they shall be comforted."
Matthew 5:4

The beatitudes of the Sermon on the Mount have a distinctive literary form called a beatitude. There are some 44 such beatitudes in the New Testament as follows:

28 in Matthew and Luke
2 in John
3 in Paul's letters to the Romans
2 in James
2 in 1 Peter
7 in Revelation

The content consists of the blessing and description for the recipient, usually identified by an attitude of conduct befitting the blessing.

Someone has called the beatitudes a sort of title page to the teachings of Jesus. The first beatitude points out the doorway into the Christian life. "Blessed are the poor in spirit for theirs is the kingdom of heaven." The first step we have to take is the fact that we are in spiritual poverty and that we are utterly bankrupt of any spiritual assets that would make us acceptable to God.

The second beatitude says, "Blessed are they that mourn: for they shall be comforted." The first application of this is that those who sense their complete spiritual bankruptcy mourn over their lost condition and are comforted with forgiveness. Also, this beatitude says that God, who is pure love, wishes to comfort all of those who mourn, whatever their needs as described below:

Blessed are they that mourn for they shall be comforted.

Blessed are they that voluntarily share their neighbors' pain.

Blessed are they who know what sorrow means.

Blessed are they who understand the sadness of others.

Blessed are they who care deeply for the problems of others.

Blessed are they who are deeply concerned about the events of this world.

Blessed are they whose burdens of life press so heavily that they give way to tears.

Blessed are they when discouragement and despair has taken over their lives.

Blessed are they who, in desperation, oppression, loneliness, bereavement, discouragement, anxiety, earnestness, present their needs to God. Then God commissions the angels of heaven to dry tears from their eyes.

Blessed are they who can feel others' needs. Old folk prayed, "Give us that love that runs from heart to heart and breast to breast."

There is a blessing in sorrow because it gives room for the Lord to administer comfort. The promise of comfort is the announcement of divine intervention. The time of remorse, disenfranchisement, loss, or bereavement is over since God will act on behalf of those who turn to Him in order to restore that lost relationship. Our confidence in God's future intervention is based on the fact that He is now at work in Jesus working beyond our capacities.

Our grief is blessed, for they are our points of contact with the divine comforter. Our mourning tears bring happiness and comfort because there is someone who understands our tears. Jesus understands!

A poet wrote, "Someone to care, someone to share all your troubles like none other can do. He'll come down from the sky, wipe the tears from your eyes; you're His child, and He cares for you." Psalm 126:5 states, "They that sow in tears shall reap in joy." Blessed are they that mourn.

Blessed are they who are grieved by sin and tried by the evils of the time. Blessed are they who demonstrate an anguish for sin, first of all, their own and, secondly, the world that is responsible for so much evil suffering. Those who mourn for their sin shall be comforted. The comfort of forgiveness is available to all who confess their sins. This is the point of reconciliation. 1 John 1:9 affirms, "If we confess our sins, he is faithful and just to forgive us our sins, and to cleanse us from all unrighteousness."

The need for reconciliation began with sin. Sin is different because it made us estranged from God. To be estranged from God is to mourn and to be sad. My father says, "God doesn't have to do anything to you, just leave you alone." When God leaves you alone, you have to mourn.

To mourn is something that is of necessity, for being poor in spirit is quite inevitable. As we look at God and His holiness and contemplate, we recognize that we are meant to live, and we see ourselves, our utter troubles, because when the church extends her loving arms, it seems that we get used. Those we help never take time to thank God or the church. Jesus was faced with the same problem as demonstrated in the story of the ten lepers.

I know it gets discouraging to keep on helping, especially if it goes unappreciated, but I stop long enough to tell you, the Lord knows. The Lord sees, and then the Lord understands. So, Jesus basically said, "When you mourn over the conditions around, you will be blessed." The wise preacher

Solomon said, "Cast your bread upon the waters for after many days you will find it again" (Ecclesiastes 11:1). My father says, "It will come back with butter on it."

Sister Brown says, "Not only will it come back with butter on it, but the Lord will sweeten it with a little jelly." Not only blessed are they that mourn, but blessed are they that mourn, for they shall be comforted.

Jesus said those who mourn have the assurance that they will be comforted. The mourning is only temporary. Mourning will only last for a season. "Weeping may endure for a night, but joy cometh in the morning." The tears will be wiped away. John said, "and God shall wipe away all tears from their eyes and there shall be no more death, neither sorrow, nor crying, neither shall there be any more pain for the former things are passed away." Thomas More said, "Here bring your wounded hearts, here tell your anguish, earth has no sorrow that heaven cannot heal."

"Blessed are they that mourn: for they shall be comforted." The Bible is replete with God's divine "shallness."

Psalm 23:1 - "The Lord is my shepherd; I shall not want."

Psalm 27:1 - "The Lord is my light and my salvation; whom shall I fear?"

Psalm 34:12 - "I will bless the Lord at all times: his praise shall continually be in my mouth. My soul shall make her boast in the Lord: the humble shall hear..."

Psalm 37:1-2,4 - "Fret not thyself because of evildoers... for they shall soon be cut down like the grass... Delight thyself also in the Lord: and he shall give thee the desires of thine heart."

Isaiah 40:31 - "But they that wait upon the Lord shall renew their strength..."

Proverbs 3:5-6 - "Trust in the Lord with all thine heart... In all thy ways acknowledge him, and he shall direct thy paths."

Isaiah 9:6 - "For unto us a child is born, unto us a son is given and the government will be upon his shoulder: and his name shall be called Wonderful."

Isaiah 40:8 - "The grass withereth, the flower fadeth: but the word of our God shall stand for ever."

Isaiah 40:4-5 - "Every valley shall be exalted, and every mountain and hill shall be made low: and the crooked shall be made straight, and the rough places plain: And the glory of the Lord shall be revealed, and all flesh shall see it together."

Romans 10:13 - "For whosoever shall call upon the name of the Lord shall be saved."

Matthew 1:21 - "And she shall bring forth a son, and thou shalt call his name Jesus: for he shall save his people from their sins."

Matthew 1:23 - "Behold, a virgin shall be with child, and shall bring forth a son, and they shall call his name Emmanuel, which being interpreted is, God with us."

Revelation 21:4 - "And God shall wipe all tears from their eyes."

1 John 3:2 - "Beloved, now are we the sons of God, and it doth not yet appear what we shall be: but we know that when he shall appear, we shall be like him; for we shall see him as he is."

THE SERMON ON THE MOUNT

"Blessed are they which do hunger and thirst after righteousness: for they shall be filled."

Matthew 5:6

Mr. Barclay calls this beatitude, "the bliss of a starving spirit." "Blessed are those who hunger and thirst for righteousness, for they will be filled." The hunger referred to in this beatitude is no gentle hunger which could be satisfied with a mid-morning snack or a sumptuous dinner. The thirst is not thirst which could be quenched with a cup of coffee, ice water, or cold drink.

It is man who is starving for spiritual food. It is the thirst of a man who will die unless he drinks from the fountain that never runs dry. "Blessed are they which do hunger and thirst after righteousness: for they shall be filled," not self-righteousness. Some people are so morally good that they have set themselves up as the high sheriff over the moral debt of the church. They talk about what they don't do. Some stop because time brings them to a halt. Some people are so heavenly bound that they are no earthly good. "Thereof, go forth as brightness and the salvation thereof as a lamp that burneth."

Hosea 10:12 states, "Sow to yourselves in righteousness, reap in mercy; break up your fallow ground: for it is time to seek the Lord, till he come and rain righteousness upon you." Matthew 6:33 declares, "But seek ye first the kingdom of God, and his righteousness; and all these things shall be added unto you." Matthew 5:20 affirms, "For I say unto you, That except your righteousness shall exceed the righteousness of the scribes and Pharisees, ye shall in no case enter into the kingdom of heaven." Romans 8:4 postulates, "That the righteousness of the law might be fulfilled in us, who walk not after the flesh, but after the Spirit." Romans 14:17 says, "For the kingdom of God is not meat and drink; but righteousness, and peace, and joy in the Holy Ghost." Philippians 1:11 declares, "Being filled with the fruits of righteousness, which are by Jesus Christ, unto the glory and praise of God." Ephesians 5:9 asserts, "(For the fruit of the spirit is in all goodness and righteousness and truth)." Blessed are they which do hunger and thirst after righteousness.

Some people don't mean to be or do right. I don't care what you do and how you treat them; they don't mean you any good. They just don't mean to do and be right. When someone doesn't like you, you can't do enough to satisfy them. If you do anything, you have done too much. If you don't do anything, you have not done enough. If you are friendly, you are said to be a flirt. If you are not friendly, then you are stuck up. If you try to come to church and try to live right, you are labeled "holier than thou." If you don't try to live holy, you are described as a hypocrite, a phony, a put on, a pretender. If you wear nice clothes, you are said to be a show-off. If you demonstrate no tendency for style, then you are a disgrace. If you work hard and try to educate your children, some people declare that you think you are better than everybody else. If you don't try to educate your children, you've got the worst children in town. If you live in a nice house and drive a decent car, some people say you are stuck on yourself. If you don't have a nice house and car, you are a menace to society. If you love church and support your pastor, you are a pastor lover and a "yes" man. If you don't support your pastor, some say you are a preacher fighter. If you go to college, get an education, some will describe you as a "know-it-all." If you don't go to college, you are classified as ignorant. If you go wild with the crowd, they say you are what's happening with the in-crowd. If you don't follow the in-crowd, some will say you are a square, coward, L-seven, dud, a firecracker that doesn't go pop, and a party pooper. If you go to school and get an education, some will say you are sophisticated. If you don't go to school, you are a drop-out. When you are young and run around with every boy and girl in town, this is called date insurance. If you don't run around, then you are called brainwashed. But, I want you to know it is not brainwashed; it is "soul washed." If they say you tell everybody all of your business, you're crazy, and should have better sense, but if you don't, they say you are stuck up. If you are a pastor and try to pastor with the Lord's help the best you know, some will say you are being a big shot. If you don't pastor effectively, you are a disgrace to the ministry.

Jesus said, "Blessed are they which do hunger and thirst after righteousness for they shall be filled." Hunger and thirst are appetites that return frequently. We often hear people say, "I was so hungry, I almost starved to death." We hear people say, "I was so thirsty, I thought I was going to pass out." When Jesus uttered these words, this is what I concluded that He meant: "Blessed are they who are starved to death. Blessed are they who almost pass out for righteousness sake, for they shall be satisfied. They shall be filled." "Blessed are they which do hunger and thirst after righteousness."

Listen to the other versions and editions that express this beatitude. "Blessed are they which do hunger and thirst for goodness." (Moffit) "Blessed are they which hunger and thirst for uprightness" (Goodspeed). "Blessed are they which hunger and thirst for being and doing right" (Williams). "Blessed are they which hunger and thirst for justice" (Lamsa). "Blessed are they which hunger and thirst for holiness" (Know). "Blessed are they which hunger and thirst to see right prevail" (New English Bible).

"Blessed are those whose heart's desire is for righteousness" (Basic English Bible). "Blessed and fortunate and happy and spiritually prosperous (that is, in that state in which the born-again child of God enjoys his favor and salvation) are those who hunger and thirst for righteousness (uprightness and right standard with God)" (Amplified).

The Gospel writer is saying to us, blessed are they who want righteousness as a hungry man wants food and a thirsty man wants water. When we hunger and thirst after righteousness, then we know that God is a fountain. We can bring the vessels of our desires to the fountain, and the Lord will fill them.

Righteousness, in the Sermon on the Mount, is soteriological. Righteousness connotes the gift of a new relationship between God and the individual. Righteousness is ethical. In this concept, righteousness connotes the demand for conduct in keeping the will of God seen in relationship to others and to God. This conduct is concomitant with the gift.

Righteousness is eschatological or Christological; righteousness expresses the new relationship that one has with God and with others. In view of Jesus' ministry, it expresses the commensurate conduct growing out of this relationship demanded by Jesus. Righteousness is a state of the heart, an attitude of the soul, the increasing aspirations after goodness conforming to God's Law. "Blessed are they which do hunger and thirst after righteousness: for they shall be filled."

They shall be filled immediately. We know when we are filled, and we know it for ourselves. The Christian is the person who knows he/she has been forgiven. He/she knows that he/she is covered by the righteousness of Jesus Christ. "Therefore, being justified by faith, we have peace with God." The Christian has this immediate feeling. The Christian is completely satisfied. The righteousness of Christ is imputed to him/her, and he/she knows that his/her sins are forgiven. The Christian knows that Christ, by the Holy Spirit, dwells within him. Christians are filled with the Holy Spirit. The Holy Spirit is in us. We are complete in Jesus Christ. When we hunger and thirst after righteousness, the Lord will fill us with His presence and His power through the Holy Spirit, as Acts 2 affirms. "Blessed are they which do hunger and thirst after righteousness: for they shall be filled." When the Lord gives life with His Holy Spirit, He fills us up and not out. Blessed are they who are spirit-filled. They shall be filled. To be filled means to put in as much as you can, as much as can be held, to heap, to load, to pack, to press down, to plug up the space in a container. To be filled means to fill up the cracks and crevices, to close up, to occupy the whole of, to be filled within and throughout, to satisfy, to imbue, to permeate, pervade, suffuse, to gratify, indulge, appease, and to pacify. "They shall be filled." They shall have their whole soul replenished. They shall be strengthened.

What do you mean? They shall have as much as can be held. They shall be supplied with a full compliment. They shall be swelled. They shall be raised to another level. They shall have the chinks covered. They shall have the crevices or pores filled. They shall be satisfied. They shall be fulfilled to its fullest. They shall be occupied. They shall be spread all the way through. They shall be overflowed. They shall be fully developed. They shall be adequate. They shall be full measure. They shall be filled to the brim. They shall be running over. They shall be extended beyond the allotted space. They shall be able to extend beyond the normal limit. They shall be able to go beyond the boundary lines. They shall have abundant provisions. They shall have plenty. They shall have their needs satisfied with the righteousness for which they longed.

When man sinned in the garden, the fellowship was broken, and communication was severed. Man was not even on the same level with God. Adam was unrighteous, and his relationship was cut off. He longed to be right with God. He longed to have the righteousness of God imputed to him.

When man sinned in the Garden of Eden, a council was called in glory, and the question was asked, "Who is worthy to go on man's bond?" Justice had decreed that, if man sinned, he would die. Jesus said, "Father, prepare me a body that will shed forth blood and water. I'll catch the nine months train and get off at Bethlehem of Judea. I'll heal the sick and raise the dead. I'll give sight to blinded eyes. I'll cause helpless cripples to throw their crutches away. I'll preach deliverance to the captives, and I'll bind up the broken hearted. I'll go to Calvary and die until justice is satisfied."

Friday, they put a rugged cross on His shoulder. Friday, they started Him up Calvary's rugged brow. Friday, they nailed His hands. Friday, they riveted His feet. Friday, they pierced Him in the side. Friday, they raised Him from a dead level to a living perpendicular on the square. Friday, they cast comical genuflections and said, "Goody, goody, we got Him now." Friday, the sun veiled its face and refused to shine. Friday, the moon hemorrhaged and ran down in blood. Friday, God turned His back on His only begotten Son. Jesus cried out, "My God, my God, why has thou forsaken me?" Friday, the angels could not minister. They said, "At your birth, we made the announcement to lowly shepherds. In the wilderness when Satan tempted You, we sustained You. We can't step in, but if You can hold on until Sunday morning, we'll be there to roll the stone away. We'll be there to make the announcement that You are risen as You said."

WORSHIPING THE LORD IN THE SPIRIT

Psalm 95:1-7; John 4:23-24

It has been often said, and it is true, that man is incurably religious. Someone has said that, if there were no God, man would be found trying to make one.

History and experience testify to the fact that there is something deeply embedded in man known as the soul, which is forever searching, reaching, and longing for a higher power. Nothing less than himself or equal to himself ever satisfies the longing of man's soul. There is an undying hunger and thirst on the inside of man that renders him inescapable of that longing in his soul.

God has set eternity in man's heart, mind, and soul, and there is no way for him to escape that thought; however, there are those who try. The soul is akin to God, and it will not rest until it finds God.

Although a man may outwardly pretend that he doesn't believe in a Supreme Being and that nothing bothers him on the inside, deep down in his heart, there is an aching void, an emptiness. There is a spiritual ear in every human heart that gives meaning to the words of the psalmist who said in his song, "Deep calleth unto deep." The depths of the human should call to the depths of divine mercy.

There is an awareness in man that is above him and beyond him; there is a higher power. He is ever conscious of the fact that there is some divine intelligence before it all and in it all. No man ever attains to such heights of intelligence and earthly enlightenment by constant study and by diligent search and research so that his thoughts of a higher power disintegrate.

So long as the mind wonders in the abiding presence of mystery and the heart hungers in the presence of infinity and the soul trembles in the presence of perfectivity, man's soul will always yearn for communion with its Maker.

When you hear a man arguing a case against God, you don't have to argue with him. He has already proven that passage of scripture which says, "The fool hath said in his heart, There is no God." Any man who argues against the existence of God is fighting a losing battle:

There is too much in man...

There is too much to man...

There is too much about man...

There is too much with man...

There is too much around man...
There is too much above man...
There is too much beneath man...

And, there is too much for man, even for the atheist to argue that there is no God. There is too much God in the world about man to be ignored by man.

Recognizing what and who God is in His divine perfections, eternal being, and the absoluteness of His holiness, together with all of His other attributes—both communicable and incommunicable, the poet wrote these immortal lines:

"The heavens declare the glory of God
And the firmaments showeth his handiwork
Day after day uttereth speech
And night unto night showeth knowledge
There is no speech or language
Where their voice is not heard."

Over and above and beyond all that, the eternal God stands eternally glorious in His own divine excellence. The Old Testament prophets and sages had no problem in identifying the eternal God from the idol gods. They knew the difference between Dagon of the Philistines and the God of Israel. They knew the difference between the God of heaven and the gods of the Amorites. They knew the difference between Jehovah and Baal. They did not confuse Elohim with Zeus (Greek god). They had no trouble distinguishing El Shaddai from the goddess Ashtoreth of the Semites. They built no shrines to Diana of the Ephesians. They didn't bow before the great image that Nebuchadnezzar set up on the plains of Dura.

They were not devotees of the gods of the Gergashites. They knew Yaweh from Minerva. They knew El Elyon from the sacred cows of China. They knew Jehovah-Jireh from the sun gods. I tell you again, the Old Testament prophets knew the eternal God.

Abraham, the father of the faithful and friend of God, erected an altar of worship to Him wherever he went and worshiped at those altars. Though crude they were, God had respect for those altars and accepted Abraham's offerings and sacrifices and accounted his faith unto him as being his righteousness.

Job bowed in reverence to God and worshiped before Him every day, even in his trying and darkest hours when life tumbled in on him. With his wife, health, children, and possessions gone, as well as friends, he held fast his integrity, saying, "Though He slay me, yet will I trust in Him."

Somewhere along the line, we have lost the meaning of true worship. Somewhere, we need to make an adjustment in our worship and in our church life as Christians. We need to shift from formality to sincerity. We need to shift from sophistication to dedication. We need to shift from pretension to being real. We need to shift from talking religion to walking religion. We need to shift from divisiveness to Christian oneness. We need to shift from being clannish to being true soldiers of the cross. We need to shift from seeking social prestige and popularity to praying for spiritual power. We need to switch from entertainment to empowerment. We need to shift from wavering to stability. We need to shift from cowardice to brave soldiers of Jesus Christ. We need to shift from boasting to bowing. We need to shift from garb wearing to cross bearing. We need a shift from robes to righteousness. We need a shift from buddies to brothers and sisters. We need a shift from gossiping to witnessing. We need a shift from membership to discipleship.

Somewhere in our Christianity, we need to make a shift, I tell you. If one would truly worship, he/she must first consider the worthiness of God and His Christ.

Oratory is not worship.

Flowery speeches do not win God's approval.

Dialogue is not worship.

Recitation of creeds is not worship.

Reading copied prayers is not worship.

Long prayers do not cause God to raise His head or lift an eyebrow.

True worship must come from the heart. You cannot worship God in self, even if you have the sweetest voice under heaven. You cannot worship God if praise is your expectation. You cannot worship God with a high mind or with a haughty spirit. You cannot bow in reverence to God and parade up and down the aisles of the church to be seen.

The essence of the matter is that worshiping God in the Spirit is acknowledging the worthiness of God in all of His magnificence, majesty, and magnanimous creativity demonstrated in His creation, including us as the highest manifestation of His work.

We cannot worship God and watch everything that goes on and see what everybody else has on. We cannot worship God with hate in our hearts. We cannot worship God and be mad with anybody. We cannot worship God, knowing we have deliberately hurt someone. We cannot worship God with green-eyed jealousy and putting on a demonstration. We cannot worship God with a grudge against our brother or sister in Christ. We cannot worship God with an evil disposition. We cannot worship God with a self-righteous attitude. We cannot worship God with a domineering spirit. We cannot worship God with a deceitful heart. We cannot worship God with a narrow mind. We cannot worship God with a holier-than-thou attitude.

We cannot worship God with a spirit of bigotry. We cannot worship God without acknowledging and confessing our sins before God. We cannot worship until we repent of our sins and beg for mercy and forgiveness at the feet of God. We cannot worship God without a clean conscience, and repentance is the only way to have it. We cannot worship God in spiritual blindness. We cannot worship God in sins' darkness. We cannot worship God without the love of God. We cannot worship without love for God. We cannot worship God without a relationship with Him.

I tell you again, true worship must come from the heart. It must come from the very bottom of the soul. If one is to truly worship God, he must first consider the worship of God. He must feel and know that he is in the presence and under the all-discerning eyes of God. We cannot worship God in self. We cannot worship God if we only enjoy our special friends on the program. We are not in worship if we can talk, talk, and talk during the service. We cannot worship God intoxicated. We cannot worship God unless we know God. We cannot worship God without faith in God. We cannot worship God without Calvary's cross. We cannot worship God and miss the crucifixion. We cannot worship God and miss the resurrection. We cannot worship God and bypass the empty tomb. We cannot worship God and miss the ascension of Christ. We cannot worship God if we do not have hope of the return of Christ.

We cannot worship God unless it is sanctioned by the Holy Spirit. We are not in worship if we come to church Sunday after Sunday to be entertained by the choir. The business of worship calls for sincerity. It calls for humility and soul searching. It calls for the prayer of thanksgiving. It calls for dedication and often re-dedication. It calls for consecration and devotion. It calls for Christian oneness.

When we come together for worship; we come for worship and not for a show. God is not interested in our shows. If God wanted a show, He could call the winds and they would put on a whistling contest which would be more pleasing and acceptable to Him and all heaven than our shows.

The psalmist said, "O come, let us worship and bow down: let us kneel before the Lord our maker... O magnify the Lord with me, and let us exalt his name together."

Let all the host of heaven worship before Him. Let men bow on their knees and worship Him. "Let the redeemed of the Lord say so." Let the heavens rejoice. Let the waters of the sea be glad. Let the fowl of the air cherub out their praise. Praise Him sun, moon, and stars. Let the thunder roar out its praise. Let all angels bow before Him in worship. Praise God in the heights above and praise Him from the depths below. Praise and worship Him from the rising of the sun unto the going down of the same.

Worship Him in His holy hills. Worship Him in the magnificent temples. Worship Him in the synagogues. Worship Him under the brush harbors. Worship God because of His holiness. Worship before Him with spiritual reverence. Praise Him for His mighty acts. Praise Him for His wonderful works. Let the saints of God say, "Amen" in worship.

Let Mt. Zion rejoice in worship. Let all the hosts of heaven worship before Him. Let all men bow on their knees and worship, "For the Lord God omnipotent reigneth." "O sing unto the Lord a new song: sing unto the Lord, all the earth. Sing unto the Lord, and bless his name; show forth his salvation from day to day. Declare his glory among the heathen... for the Lord is great, and greatly to be praised." He is to be feared among all gods. "Honor and majesty are before Him, and strength and beauty are in His Sanctuary."

WALKING IN THE SPIRIT
Galatians 5:16-18

Charles Stanley in his book, *The Wonderful Spirit Filled Life*, says, "For too many believers, the Christian life boils down to simply doing the best they can." There is no dynamic, no power, and there is no real distinctive that can be attributed to anything other than discipline and determination. Many believers' doctrine can be summed up in two statements:

1. Nobody's perfect
2. God understands

As a result, life is void of the divine.

The real tragedy is that we have lost our ability to function in our society the way God originally intended. Tony Evans says, "Our lives are to be a commercial announcement of a coming Kingdom; people should be able to look at us and know there is something different about us." It is not our clothes, or our hairstyle, but us. What is on the inside...

There should be something different in the way we do business. We are the only Jesus most people will ever know.

The tragedy is, no wonder that so many non-Christians want nothing to do with Christ or His Church. The reason is, they know too many so-called Christians. God's method for reaching this generation is Christians whose lifestyles are empowered and directed by the Holy Spirit. The apostle John refers to the Holy Spirit as being given to the believers (1 John 3:24). Peter talks about the Holy Spirit being in believers (1 Peter 1:11). Paul says, "God hath sent forth the Spirit of his Son into your hearts," in Galatians 4:6. In 1 Corinthians 3:16-17, he speaks of the believer as the Temple of the Holy Spirit. All of these terms lead us in the same direction. The Holy Spirit resides in the believer. The verb used most often to describe this unique relationship comes from the Greek word *oikeo*. In the *New American Standard Bible*, it is translated dwell, indwell, and to live.

In the *King James Version*, it is translated dwell. *Oikeo* actually comes from the Greek word for house. It means, to live in or reside.

The significance of the term *oikeo* is that it speaks of permanency. The idea is that the Holy Spirit takes up residency in believers forever. He doesn't just pass through; He makes us His home, and He comes to stay.

When the Holy Spirit is in our lives, it is *sessile*, permanent. He is an eternal inhabitant. Having grown up a devout Jew, Paul had a great deal of respect for the Temple. To the nation of Israel, it represented the presence of

God among His people. When Christ was crucified, there was no longer any need for the Temple. God no longer needed a building. He was free to take up residency in the hearts of man.

The barrier of sin had been removed. Man's relationship with God had been restored. To symbolize the change, God tore the veil of the Temple from top to bottom (Mark 15:38). The veil was drapery separating the Holy of Holies from the rest of the Temple. The fact that it was ripped from the top to bottom signified that God, not man, initiated the change. By referring to believers as Temples, Paul was announcing that God had changed His residency for good. He had left the Temple in Jerusalem and, through the person of the Holy Spirit, had moved into the hearts of His people.

In every believer, there is a conflict, which is expressed graphically for us in Galatians 5:16-25. Here, we have two contrasting elements in our lives— the flesh on the one side and the Holy Spirit on the other side. These are in direct contrast to each other. They are two opposing sources from which expressions of conduct flow. If we live our own lives, we express the flesh. If we live the Christ life, it is because of the Holy Spirit within us. The flesh and the Spirit are the basic terms of our identification with the human family, on the one hand, or with our divine family on the other. To live after flesh is our identification with the human family, with Adam as our forefather. If we live after Spirit, that is our identification with the divine family, which is born of God.

In Adam, we all inherit the flesh. In Christ, those who place their trust in Him inherit the Holy Spirit. The desires of the flesh are opposed to the desires of the Spirit, and the desires of the Spirit are opposed to the flesh. As long as this conflict is unresolved in us, we cannot do the things that we need to do. The flesh or the old nature, the fallen nature from Adam, is in every believer, as long as we dwell in these unredeemed bodies.

It is the flesh. The Holy Spirit is also within us. The Spirit, He has been given to every believer. The Holy Spirit is there to subdue and conquer the flesh nature so that we can be free to do the will of God. A mistake made by many Christians is that we try to gain victory over the flesh by our own will and efforts. We are trying to overcome the flesh by using the flesh. The way of deliverance then is to walk in the Spirit (v. 16), we are led by the Spirit (v. 18), and we are to live in the Spirit (v. 25).

When man was created, He was created a living soul. He was provided with a mind; someone has called it the calculator. He was given emotions; someone has called them the reactor. And, He also had the will, which has been called the executor. In the life of Christians, the flesh and the Spirit seek to control the mind, the emotions, and the will.

The question comes, how is it possible that the flesh still has such a strong pull on the believer's life? How can the Holy Spirit cohabit the same body with the unholy flesh?

The Scriptures teach that the true believer is no longer in the flesh but in the Spirit (Romans 8:1-9). How then does the flesh continue to operate in the believer's life along side the Spirit?

Lloyd Jones suggests, "My old self, that self that was in Adam, was an utter slave to sin. When I accept Jesus Christ, I have a new self. I am a new man, a new creature. I am not doing this or that. It is the sin that remains in my members that does so. Sin is no longer in me. In my new self; it is in my members only." This sin that remains in me, Lloyd Jones called it "The Flesh." The flesh, says Neil Anderson, is the tendency within each person to operate independently of God and to center his interest on himself. An unsaved person functions totally in the flesh (Romans 8:7-8), worshiping and serving the creature more than the Creator (Romans 1:25). But when you were born again, your old self died, and your new self came to life. But during the years you spent separated from God, your worldly experiences thoroughly programmed your brain with thoughts, patterns, memory, traces, responses, habits, all of which are alien to God. So, even though your old man is gone, your flesh remains in opposition to God. The flesh—*sarx*, a Greek word translated flesh—refers to the physical body. *Sarx* is used also to refer to human effort. Man's efforts to accomplish the supernatural by natural means *sarx*, which refers to our unredeemed nature. It is the flesh, where sin resides, and it also has the effect on the mind. It is the part of us that encompasses your body, feelings, thoughts, mind, and any part of you that is tainted by sin (Romans 7:15).

In salvation, one's spirit is changed and made new, but the new man remains in an old house. Psychology and pragmatism represent fleshly attempts to solve spiritual problems. Every problem in life comes from the flesh; every solution comes from the Spirit. There is a Greek word *prolambano*. It means, trapped, bound by, or in bondage to. There is another Greek word, *paraptoma* which carries the idea of falling or stumbling into sin. So, when a believer falls and is caught in sin, the spiritual are to act. The need is for restoration. The verb *katartizo* means to restore, to mend, to repair.

The flesh is in disrepair, and the spiritual are called to come and help repair it. Paul said we are to walk in the Spirit, which means we are to order our manner of life and behavior in conformity with the Holy Spirit. Wuest says, "When the flesh presses hard upon the believer with its evil behests, the Holy Spirit is there to oppose the flesh and give the believer victory over it, in order that the believer will not obey the flesh. God's provision is such that man has been set free from the Law, free from bondage, of the old nature, free to depend upon the Holy Spirit, so that he can create the life of Christ with in us."

So, the admonition is to walk in the Spirit, which means, walking in the Spirit a step at a time. In this way, we will not fulfill the lusts of the flesh.

1 John 1:6-10—If we say that we have fellowship with him, and walk in darkness, we lie, and do not the truth: But if we walk in the light, as he is in the light, we have fellowship one with another, and the blood of Jesus Christ his Son cleanseth us from all sin. If we say that we have no sin, we deceive ourselves, and the truth is not in us. If we confess our sins, he is faithful and just to forgive us our sins, and to cleanse us from all unrighteousness. If we say that we have not sinned, we make him a liar, and his word is not in us.

I. Walking in the Spirit Is a Priceless Privilege
Our sins are:
1. Blotted out (Isaiah 43:25; 44:22; Acts 3:19)
2. Borne by another (1 Peter 2:24)
3. Cast behind God's back (Isaiah 38:17)
4. Covered (Romans 4:7)
5. Cast into the depths of the sea (Micah 7:19)
6. Finished (Daniel 9:24)
7. Forgiven (Colossians 2:13)
8. Not beheld (Numbers 23:21)
9. Not imputed (Romans 4:8)
10. Not remembered (Hebrews 8:12)
11. Pardoned (Micah 7:18)
12. Passed away (Zechariah 3:4)
13. Purged (Hebrews 1:3)
14. Put away (Hebrews 7:27)
15. Remitted (Acts 10:43)
16. Removed (Psalm 103:12)
17. Subdued (Micah 7:19)
18. Sought for and not found (Jeremiah 50:20)
19. Washed away with blood (1 John 1:7)
20. Taken away (Isaiah 27:9)

When we walk in the Spirit:
Saints are edified.
Lives are changed.
Burdens are lifted.

Cares are eliminated.
Temptations are overcome.
Needs are met.
Bodies are healed.
Souls are enriched.
Nerves are settled.
Differences are dissolved.
Doubts are destroyed.
Fears are banished.
Hearts are touched.
Problems are solved.
Blessings are enjoyed.
Questions are answered.
Ministries are inspired.
Demons are overthrown.
Frustrations are abolished.
Emotions are stirred.
Confusions are cleared.
Minds are enlightened.
Sorrows are removed.
Spirits are revived.
Joys are revered.
Hopes are restored.
Decisions are made.
Angels are excited.
Sins are forgiven.

II. When We Walk in the Spirit, We Have a Positive Promise
John 14:18 - I will not leave you comfortless: I will come to you.
When the Holy Spirit controls our lives, then the Holy Spirit:
1.   Reveals things in men
2.   Comes into our midst
3.   Instructs men
4.   Testifies to us
5.   Can judge and purge
6.   Lifts up the standard against Satan
7.   Makes men full of power
8.   Leads, guides
9.   Casts out devils
10. Quickens
11. Flows like a river
12. Will teach all things

13. Will bring to our remembrance
14. Dwells in believers
15. Makes us free from sin and death
16. Bears witness of our sonship
17. Helps us pray
18. Works miracles in our lives
19. Imparts love
20. Makes new creatures
21. Imparts gifts
22. Baptizes believers into the body of Christ (the Church)
23. Gives life
24. Gives liberty—sets free
25. Changes lives
26. Is the source of our hope
27. Imparts character
28. Gives fellowship
29. Strengthens the inner man
30. Is the source of sanctification and holiness (Romans 12:1-2)
31. Invites men to God
32. Transforms and reforms
33. Is the administrator of the affairs of the saints
34. Is the comforter
35. Is the Giver of Life—at the moment of regeneration, we are made recipients of the Holy Spirit. If any man have not the Spirit of Christ, he is none of His. (Romans 8:9)

III. When We Walk in the Spirit, We Have Purifying Power

1. The command is in the imperative mood. You be filled with the Spirit. The imperative mood demands obedience.

2. The verb "be filled" is the plural form. He is saying to all of us, individually and collectively, that we, as a universal body of Christ, must be filled with the Holy Spirit.

3. It is in the passive voice. "Be filled," is the command to fill yourself up with the Spirit. *The New English Bible* renders this verse, "Let the Holy Spirit fill you."

4. The command to be filled is in the present tense. It is a continuous appropriation, not some great, once-in-a-lifetime moment. What we are saying, Lord, is this is Your day. As each moment unfolds, I want to walk with You, allowing Your Spirit full control.

The word translated walking in Greek, *peripateo*, which means go about.

Walk means go about, walk around, live, conduct. This Greek word, *peripateo* comes from the Hebrew word *halak*, which means walk or conduct; it has to do with one's life. The present tense of the imperative is *peripateite*, which denotes an exhortation to action in progress. Paul is saying to the Galatians, they are to continue doing what they are already doing, a habitual pattern that is step by step, day by day, relying on His power and direction, experiencing the presence and the power of the Spirit working in their lives, and living by faith. The way to victory over the flesh is this process:

1.   Living
2.   Walking
3.   Being led by the Holy Spirit

On the computer is the Help key, an Escape key, and then there is the Control-Alt-Delete. When nothing else works, punch the Control-Alt-Delete, and start all over again. When you get stuck and nothing else is moving, punch Control-Alt-Delete. When you walk with God and it seems like you get bogged down, when you press Help and Escape and still can't get moving, punch Control-Alt-Delete, and start all over again.

When God is in control, He gives purifying power.

There is a word:

Integrate—From the root word we get the word integrity, which means to form or blend into a whole, to unite or to be unique. When we walk in the Spirit, there is integrity, there is a blend. We are united in the Spirit; there is a filling.

Filled is the Greek word *pletho*, which means furnished completely or lacking nothing. Literally, it means free from starvation, want, or desire. When we are filled with the Holy Spirit, the believer is brought into a Spirit of accuracy and exactness. The exactness of Christ. When you go the airport and go through the metal detector, sometimes scanners, you have to take out keys, credit cards, jewelry, change. When we walk in the Spirit, we have to go through God's metal detector and take out every sin, hate, malice, jealousy, envy, strife. In Ephesians 5:18, we read, "And do not be drunk with wine, in which is dissipation; but be filled with the Spirit." In this verse, there are two commands: The first is negative, "Do not be drunk with wine." The second is positive, "But be filled with the Spirit."

❧N   O   T   E   S❧

❧NOTES❧

❧ N O T E S ❧

❧ N O T E S ❧

❧ NOTES ❧